PREVIOUS BOOKS BY JEFFREY KOTTLER

Introduction to Therapeutic Counseling (with Robert Brown), Third Edition. Pacific Grove, Calif.: Brooks/Cole, 1996.

Growing a Therapist. San Francisco: Jossey-Bass, 1995.

Beyond Blame: A New Way of Resolving Conflicts in Relationships. San Francisco: Jossey-Bass, 1994.

The Heart of Healing: Relationships in Therapy (with Tom Sexton and Susan Whiston). San Francisco: Jossey-Bass, 1994.

Classrooms Under the Influence: Counteracting Problems of Addiction (with Richard Powell and Stan Zehm). Newbury Park, Calif.: Corwin Press, 1994.

The Emerging Professional Counselor: From Dreams to Realities (with Richard Hazler). Alexandria, Va.: American Counseling Association Press, 1994.

On Being a Therapist (Revised Edition). San Francisco: Jossey-Bass, 1993.

Teacher As Counselor (with Ellen Kottler). Newbury Park, Calif.: Corwin Press, 1993.

Advanced Group Leadership. Pacific Grove, Calif.: Brooks/Cole, 1993.

On Being a Teacher (with Stan Zehm). Newbury Park, Calif.: Corwin Press, 1993.

Compassionate Therapy: Working with Difficult Clients. San Francisco: Jossey-Bass, 1992.

The Compleat Therapist. San Francisco: Jossey-Bass, 1991.

Private Moments, Secret Selves: Enriching Our Time Alone. New York: Ballantine, 1990.

The Imperfect Therapist: Learning from Failure in Therapeutic Practice (with Diane Blau). San Francisco: Jossey-Bass, 1989.

Pragmatic Group Leadership. Pacific Grove, Calif.: Brooks/Cole, 1983.

Mouthing Off: A Study of Oral Behavior, Its Causes and Treatments. New York: Libra, 1981.

Ethical and Legal Issues in Counseling and Psychotherapy: A Comprehensive Guide (with William Van Hoose). San Francisco: Jossey-Bass, 1977.

the language
of tears

the language
of tears

Jeffrey A. Kottler

Jossey-Bass Publishers • San Francisco

Substantial discounts on bulk quantities of Jossey-Bass books are available to corporations, professional associations, and other organizations. For details and discount information, contact the special sales department at Jossey-Bass Inc., Publishers (415) 433–1740; Fax (800) 605–2665.

For sales outside the United States, please contact your local Simon & Schuster International office.

TCF Manufactured in the United States of America on Lyons Falls Pathfinder Tradebook. This paper is acid-free and 100 percent totally chlorine-free.

Interior and cover design by Paula Goldstein

Library of Congress Cataloging-in-Publication Data

Kottler, Jeffrey A.
    The language of tears / Jeffrey A. Kottler.
        p.   cm.
    Includes bibliographical references and index.
    ISBN 0–7879–0265–9
    1. Crying.   2. Tears—Psychological aspects.   I. Title.
BF575.C88K67   1996
152.4—dc20   96–11136

HB Printing   10 9 8 7 6 5 4 3 2 1   FIRST EDITION

contents

preface

I have become accustomed to people who are crying. Not a working day goes by when I don't encounter weeping of one sort or another—tears of despondency and hopelessness, of abject surrender, tears of sentimental reminiscence, tears of sadness and grief, tears of regret, of frustration, even the tears of laughter and joy. I have learned to recognize these various kinds of tears, to know when silence is best, or words of comfort. I know when to change the subject or when to offer a hug. I can tell when the tears are saying "Please help me!" as distinguished from those that say "Leave me alone!" or even those that say "Join me in my moment of exaltation!"

I am a therapist, an educator and supervisor of other therapists, a researcher who writes about the healing nature of human relationships. I have spent my life as a student of tears. I have sat helplessly, watching couples rip into one another with a viciousness that provokes tears of outrage or anguish. I have consoled parents whose children are dying. I have tried to help people who are so depressed their eyes have run dry; they have no tears left to give. I have watched, with rapture and pride, the tearful reconciliation of a parent and an estranged child. I have seen so many tears and heard so many sobs that crying has become as familiar to me as a frown, or even a yawn.

Yet with all this experience and practice, I am still not entirely comfortable with people who are crying, especially if I might have played some incidental role in its beginning. When my wife cries, I sit stoically, wearing my "shrink mask" and pretending to be empathic; inside, I want to run away or scream "Stop that and talk about it!" When my son cries, I want to die, though I act as if I am unperturbed, with what I hope is just the right mixture of concern and neutrality. When a student approaches me tearfully about a grade that is lower than expected, I just shut down. I put up a wall to stop melting from the heat.

When even experts on the subject struggle with their own tears, as well as responding to those of others, you can be sure that we are onto something that is vitally important in our lives, even if it is so poorly understood.

WHAT THIS BOOK WILL DO

This is a book about passion in human experience. It is a study of excruciating pain as well as exquisite rapture. There are tears of grief, sadness, despondency, hopelessness, of relief, exhilaration, pride, and ecstasy. What is the meaning of this language? What are tears for? How did they evolve? How are tears interpreted in various cultures and throughout history? How are men and women, children and adults, unique in the ways they cry? Why do some people cry so easily and others do not? When is crying therapeutic and when does it become self-destructive? What is the best way to respond to someone who is crying? And perhaps most important of all: What do tears tell us about the essence of our own human nature?

These are but a few of the questions that prompted this study of crying. Based on research conducted during the past twelve years, this book brings together the sparse literature on the subject from across all disciplines—from ophthalmology and neurology to anthropology and social psychology, from fiction and film studies to social work and counseling.

This book will broaden your understanding. Tears represent a metaphor for human feeling. There is not a person alive who has not wondered about the meaning of tears, what they say about who we are. Thousands of songs have been composed about them; almost every movie worth remembering is one that stimulated the flow of tears. Yet in spite of the fascination with this subject, very few people understand their own tears, much less those of others they are close to.

This book will move you emotionally. Although *The Language of Tears* is full of interesting information, research, and concepts, anecdotes are included that are moving, even heart wrenching in their vivid descriptions. Further, I will speak directly to you, the reader, challenging you to look deeply at your own tearful behavior as a way to understand the phenomenon on a larger scale. The goal of this book is no less than to move you to tears.

This book will change your life. It is not enough simply to understand this complex phenomenon, nor is it sufficient to feel the impact of the messages contained therein. The structure of the book, as well as its style, is designed to help you take action in your life, to confront "emotional constipation" or its counterpart of helplessness, to initiate changes in the ways you relate to others and to yourself.

In the pages that follow, you will enter the lives of many individuals who describe their tearful experiences. You will learn much of what there is to know about this mystery of human behavior. You will also have the opportunity to look inward, to examine the particular meaning that tears have had for you during your life. Finally, you will come to terms with the language of your own tears, as well as gain a better grasp of what others have been trying to communicate to you for a long time.

ACKNOWLEDGMENTS

I wish to express my gratitude to two professionals whose wisdom and guidance proved invaluable in the completion of this book. Bill Frey, of the St. Paul–Ramsey Tear Research Center, offered many suggestions that helped me to refine my ideas related to the subject of crying. I am also grateful for the support, guidance, and wisdom of Alan Rinzler, an editor who nurtures and pushes me to the limits of what I am capable of doing.

Las Vegas, Nevada   JEFFREY A. KOTTLER
June 1996

the language
of tears

1

a student of tears

Y ou are surrounded by tears. People are crying all around you, and have been throughout most of your life, just as you have been known to weep yourself on occasion. Although this phenomenon of shedding water out of your eyes during times of emotional upheaval is one of the most remarkable mysteries on this planet, most people don't understand very clearly what this behavior is for, nor why it has such a dramatic impact on others.

What a peculiar reaction is elicited by this strange form of communication! Crying is a language system that—while powerfully evocative—is all too often misunderstood. It is curious indeed how uncomfortable and embarrassed most people feel being around others, or even themselves, during tearful times.

If we adopt the role of the student, this subject opens a whole new world before us. All of a sudden, we begin to make sense of why people react the ways they do to the display of tears, and why we have responded, as well, in particular ways to the overflow of feeling that pours out of our own eyes.

As a student of tears, you will learn to recognize distinctly different messages that are being communicated by this behavior—expressions of sadness, grief, and despair; displays of elation, joy, and exaltation; releases of tension, frustration, apprehension; outpourings of anger and rage. Among all the various expressions that are part of this language, you will note shades of deception and authenticity that mask underlying feelings.

The ultimate test for any student is being able to apply newly found knowledge where it counts most: in your daily interactions with loved ones. It is not enough to be able to observe what people are doing and why they act as they do; what matters most is how you are able to respond more authentically and constructively to the presence of tears, whether in yourself or others.

BEING A STUDENT OF TEARS

Some students sit in class and daydream. They are not really interested in the subject but are just there because someone else thought it would be a good idea. Such students go through the motions. They read material as if they are studying something outside themselves rather than a subject that is part of every fiber of their being. They may or may not be conversant in the material after the class is over, but one thing is certain—it never touched them in any meaningful way. You have read hundreds of books in this way.

Another level of depth for a student is diving into a subject not only with the head but with the heart. After deciding that a subject is well worth focused attention, a book becomes part of the student's life. The student thinks continuously about the implications of the ideas for daily life.

If your intention is to do more than read this book, to

actually make the ideas contained within it a stimulus for constructive changes in the ways you think about yourself and others, some suggestions might be useful.

- STEP BACKWARD. Look at the big picture of what is going on all around you. Adopt the roles of the psychologist, sociologist, anthropologist, and student of human nature. At times, detach yourself from what is happening in the world around you or inside your own body, and apply the new principles to decipher what this behavior means.

- LOOK INWARD. If objectivity helps you to disengage from your emotional reactions so that you might see things more clearly, then subjective experience is just as valuable to help you access your innermost thoughts and feelings. This is a very personal book, dealing with the most intimate of subjects. Allow the feelings within you to be stirred up. Attend carefully to how you are reacting inside.

- BE REFLECTIVE. Ask yourself continuously about the meaning of behavior. What are my tears saying right now? Why am I not crying even though I am feeling so sad? What is it about this particular tearful episode that is so memorable when others have faded away? What cultural differences have I observed in the ways that people cry? What is this person communicating by the way he is weeping? In what ways are these tears authentic expressions of feeling, and how are they being manipulative? Over and over again, you will be asked to reflect on what crying means in various circumstances.

- EXPERIMENT WITH LETTING YOURSELF GO. As you become a more knowledgeable student of tears, one thing you may notice is that the quantity and quality of your crying may change. Some people report that something breaks loose within them, that tears that have been withheld for many years begin to flow. Others find that the intensive study of an aspect of their behavior makes them feel self-conscious, and therefore less spontaneous in the ways they express themselves. Note the changes in your own crying patterns. Trust yourself to let go.

- DRAW CONNECTIONS. Although the focus of our study is the subject of crying, this topic is connected to many other aspects of your life. Integrate what you learn in this context to things you have read and seen before. Challenge those ideas that don't seem to fit with your experience, asking yourself what that means. Make the material in this book part of you by connecting it to everything else that you know and understand. Truly active students are the ones who are not content to accept ideas uncritically; they invent their own theories.

- CHALLENGE YOURSELF. There is no sense in deceiving you—there are some very painful facets to this subject. In fact, crying is often about some of the most intense feelings you've ever had. Look carefully at these tearful times in your life. Push yourself to explore at deeper levels what your tears have been saying to you, what you have been hiding from, what you need to deal with in your life.

- TALK TO PEOPLE. Over and above what it sparks within yourself, one of the best parts of a good book is what it stimulates in your conversations with others. Tell someone you love about how you restrict your own tears, or how you feel when she is tearful. Test some of the ideas you read about by checking them out with others. Best of all, there are few questions that reveal more about a person than asking when the last time was that he cried.

You will be surprised by the reactions you get. As a student of tears, you will discover that most people are evasive, feeling quite correctly that this is among the most personal questions you could ever ask someone, one of those secret weapons that therapists use to get people to unlock the secrets of their souls. Depending on the trust that is felt, the subject of your inquiry might offer a perfunctory answer, for example, citing the emotional reaction elicited by a sad movie. With such a response, most people are being something less than honest. This is actually a contrived tearful experience, one that was carefully orchestrated by the director, even if the subject was genuine and honestly portrayed. There is little risk in revealing this to you—others in the theater were crying as well.

If you can encourage people to tell you about the last time they really cried spontaneously, when their bodies turned on the faucet before they knew what was going on, you are likely to hear a story that is unnerving in its intimacy and vulnerability. One man, for example, revealed the following incident that took him completely by surprise:

My wife and I were sitting in a cafe having a quiet lunch by the sea. We were relaxed, on vacation, enjoying the prospect of a day without structure. I honestly don't know or fully understand what triggered this episode. One minute I was trying to decide whether to slice a section of melon before I ate it, or to just pop the whole thing in my mouth, and the next instant I started crying.

I don't know who was more startled—my wife, who wondered if I had finally lost it, and on such a beautiful day too, over a melon yet—or me. Tears were streaming down my face but I was not sure why I was crying. Perhaps that was the most frightening of all.

As I became aware of the sequence of images that preceded the outburst, which by now had become quite emotional, I settled down to a steady stream of tears. At least now, to my wife's relief, I wasn't making much noise. Melon. A flash of my mother. Who loved melon. Loved. Past tense. Because she is dead. And has been for twenty years. Poor Mom. Poor me. I never really cried for my mother, never grieved fully for myself, never let myself feel the extent of my pain and loss. But why now? Why here? This is one of those times when my body said: "Enough is enough! I am tired of keeping this stuff around. If you won't deal with it, fine, I will!"

Interviewing people such as this man about tearful times facilitates greater closeness among us. We are sharing, in a sense, those experiences that have moved us the most. We are revealing the most vulnerable aspects of who we are. Thus, talking about the language of tears may very well build greater intimacy in your relationships. As a student of this subject, you become more knowledgeable about a mysterious aspect of Nature, as well as more closely connected to the people who matter the most. Most of all, you learn to become fluent in reading and speaking the language of tears in such a way that recognizes nuances you may have never sensed before.

ALL TEARS ARE NOT THE SAME

If we are to be students of tears and study this complex and mysterious language that transcends words, we must follow a process in which we first understand the various meanings that crying can have. Consequently, we will study the vocabulary of tears, the various types of crying that can exist. We will also look at how this strange reaction of excreting liquid from our eyes evolved over time.

There is a syntax and grammar to the language of tears, a set of cultural, gender, familial, genetic, and interactional rules for when and where this behavior is permitted. Ultimately, we will apply these concepts to those situations that we find most perplexing—during those times when either we are crying with little self-control or we are in the company of others who are hurting.

There are a number of ideas that I wish to introduce throughout this book, concepts that evolved from a systematic study of the research in various fields, as well as from my experiences as a student of tears over a lifetime as a therapist, supervisor and trainer of other therapists, and curious observer of my own and others' behavior.

Overflowing Emotion

Imagine an internal reservoir that stores all feelings safely in place. The level of emotional arousal constantly rises and lowers as we are subjected to various life experiences and hormonal changes, as well as perceptual interpretations. During periods of upheaval, crisis, disorientation, or shock, this system sloshes around, spilling excess water out through the eyes.

The storage capacity for each individual varies tremendously. Some people cry quite easily in response to the most mild surprises; others have an internal reservoir so cavernous that in their lifetime they can't recall a single instance when it came close to the point of spilling over. These wide individual differences in the propensity to cry are part of what make this subject so fascinating for the student. You will learn how differences in hormone levels, brain chemistry, cultural and gender conditioning, maturation and development, parental modeling, and life experiences contribute to the likelihood that any sort of emotional arousal will lead to a tearful response.

Two people, for example, have just been informed that the business proposition they had been counting on has just fallen through. Both Monica and Myla feel crestfallen, devastated. This opportunity would not only have meant a stable source of income and a major career advancement for them, but this partnership would have cemented a friendship that both were finding increasingly stimulating and supportive.

If there was a way to measure the physiological arousal going on in their endocrine systems, the hypothalamic and cortical regions of their brains, their sympathetic nervous systems, and their corresponding internal reactions, you would find virtually identical levels of stimulation. Both Monica and Myla are clearly very upset, so much so that heart rate, blood pressure, and respiration are way above normal. In addition, the cognitive activity inside their brains is following a similar course, reviewing what they did wrong, admonishing themselves for their failure, stirring up feelings of panic at the prospect of a bleak future.

More than anything else, both of them are feeling just plain sad. This may not be surprising, but you would be puzzled at how each of them is revealing so differently the overflow of emotion that is going on inside them. Monica is visibly sobbing, tears running down her cheeks with abandon. She is disappointed, angry, hurt, and discouraged; you can see these intense feelings reflected in the moisture that is now beginning to pool on her collar.

Myla reaches out to her with an arm around her shoulder. Myla's face, however, looks quite grim and tight. There is not a drop of moisture in her eyes, not a hint of despair showing on her face. Looking at her, you might not be altogether certain what she is feeling—but you can tell that *something* intense is going on inside her.

Myla is from a family background and culture in which nobody around her ever cried much when she was a child. During those times when she shed a tear or two after scraping her knee or bringing home a bad grade in school, she was teased mercilessly by her brothers and father. Crying, in Myla's experience, has always been interpreted as a sign of weakness, of surrender. She taught herself from a very young age to make her internal reservoir of emotional sensitivity quite elastic. If she were to cry, it would mean that she had all but given up in defeat, a circumstance that through sheer force of will she would simply not permit.

Tears may signal an overflow of emotion, but as can be seen in the cases of Monica and Myla, the rate and frequency of these surges depends on a number of variables unique to each individual.

Crying and Health

There is compelling evidence from research in biochemistry, neurology, and ophthalmology, as well as the social sciences, that crying, *within limits,* is an important human function. Crying not only serves a number of crucial physiological purposes like lubricating the eye and excreting toxic chemicals, but it also is important for bonding interpersonal relationships. However, just as stifling all urges toward tearful expression can be destructive to your peace of mind and intimate relationships, so too can crying in excess be unhealthy.

The balance between crying fluently, to express what you are feeling inside, but not excessively, to the point where you shut down other forms of communication, is a major theme that we will be exploring throughout the pages that follow. In the case of the two businesswomen just described, Monica feels mostly satisfied with the ways she expresses herself emotionally. She cries easily when in the presence of those she trusts, especially her siblings and closest friends like Myla. In other circumstances, such as business negotiations or social encounters with acquaintances, she finds that with concerted effort she can keep all her emotional responses, including tears, under control. She contrasts her own experience with that of her older sister, a world-class crier by her own admission. Monica recalls many times seeing her sister lose herself in her tears to the point where she just folds in on herself, driving away everyone around her.

Just as Monica's sister represents one end of the unhealthy continuum where tears become a sign of complete loss of control, Myla has restricted her own displays of feeling to the point where she is rarely in touch with what is going on inside her. In the setback described earlier, she denies the extent of her disappointment and sadness. After awhile, Monica will start to feel fairly uncomfortable that she is crying from her heart while her friend seems to be so controlled. Eventually, this difference will drive a wedge into their relationship as each one feels uneasy in the presence of the other's response, which is so foreign to her own experience.

In addition to restricting her flow of tears, Myla exhibits other symptoms of emotional constipation that are taking a toll on her health. She does not sleep well at night, even when she exercises religiously to work off excess energy. She is prone to chronic digestion problems that may or may not be related to stress in her life. Most significant, however, has been the way the levels of intimacy in her relationships with friends like Monica have been compromised by her inability (or unwillingness) to show on the outside what she is feeling on the inside. This coping strategy may have served her well growing up in her family, but she is finding again and again that others find it hard to get close to her.

Crying and Truth

When words fail us, tears will spontaneously fall, as if to say: "I know that he is too embarrassed to say so, but he really does need some help right now." Tears are thus an authentication of meaning. They communicate powerfully, forcefully, honestly what you are feeling inside. Even when they are not asking for help, tears are telling others about the essence of your experience in that moment. They are sometimes scalding hot in their intensity, other times they are almost languid in their casual arrival, but always they bring with them a sense of presence that cannot be ignored.

Even when we are uncomfortable being around people who are crying, we are struck by the drama of the event. Tears are often meant for others' view, to say something compelling that words cannot express. They lend an authenticity to communication that words cannot touch. You may doubt what people tell you, or even what they exhibit by their actions, but when tears show themselves you have no choice but to pay attention. They are the punctuation at the end of a statement that gives credence and power to what was said.

During one conversation, for example, a woman had confided to a group of friends that she had been having a hard time lately. As if reviewing a list of minor annoyances, she calmly recited one tragedy after another that had befallen her in the previous months. Her son eloped after his girlfriend became pregnant. A few weeks after their wedding, he went into a coma during a minor medical procedure. Just a few weeks after that, her father died. Then. . . .

Before she could continue, one man who had been listening began to visibly tremble. He spoke so softly to her that you could barely hear his words, which were superfluous in any event. What was absolutely riveting was the amount of effort he was exercising to hold himself back. It was so clear he was moved by this woman's narrative. Although tears had not yet emerged, his eyes were watery and his face scrunched into that indelible sign that they were not far behind.

The woman responded instantly to this empathic offering. She reached out to touch his arm, actually offering him comfort even though she was the one who had been suffering. His own emotional display acted as a catalyst for her to express more genuinely what she had been feeling all along.

Tears streamed down both her cheeks. A silent conversation was taking place between the two people, revealing to each other what was in their hearts. Neither one had the slightest doubt that what was taking place between them, in the span of a few minutes, was profoundly moving, connecting them in ways that could not have happened any other way.

In his study of the underlying meanings of various emotional expressions, psychologist Nico Frijda made the point that crying doesn't so much *express* sorrow or helplessness as it *is* these feelings in behavioral form. Far more effective than merely asking for compassion or understanding, tears demand a response that words can never touch. They elaborate meaning in a way that could never be described in verbal conversation.

Crying and Deception

Spontaneous displays of emotion that slip out, as in the case of this man and woman, are only part of the language of tears. These are unconscious, involuntary reactions that are controlled by internal neural mechanisms. The emotional reservoir reaches the point where it will burst unless there is some release.

Tearful reactions can also be initiated intentionally, just as they can be inhibited. Well-timed bouts of crying represent the ultimate in deception, playing on your sympathy to win some advantage. This works equally well when engineered by a movie actor who is trying to draw you into a story, or an amateur in your life who is attempting to control you with an effective cry. A well-timed tear can be among the most powerful ways to win sympathy or attention, to get people to back off, or to throw them off balance.

Among all animals, deception is a crucial dimension of communication. Natural selection has favored both those who are good at disguising their intentions and those who are good at spotting deception. If tears can be used to communicate more accurate representations of internal states, they can also be employed to disguise true feelings and throw people off track. Impression, after all, is everything.

So, the interesting question is not why people would ever use tears to lead others astray but rather why anyone would want others to know about feelings of vulnerability. The answer is that if others perceive you as nonthreatening (and tears are a symbol of surrender), they may very well leave you alone.

Crying on demand does not exactly require professional training. At this very moment, you could probably cry by recapturing an image of a profoundly sad or tragic time in your life. With just as little effort, and sufficient motivation, you could also stop the flow of tears. In other words, it is not always apparent when a person is crying whether the communication is genuine or contrived, whether it's a deeply felt emotion or simply an intentional display, even a manipulative ploy to win sympathy.

As a student of tears, you need to be aware that false images can be displayed for deceptive purposes. There are many reasons why you might not wish others to know what you are really feeling, perhaps a lack of trust in this particular relationship, a fear of rejection by the person, or shame over what you are thinking. Similarly, you may wish to pretend you are feeling something that you are not.

Sigmund Freud was perhaps unduly optimistic in his belief that deceptive emotions can easily be recognized. He stated confidently that to the trained observer "no mortal can keep a secret. If his lips are silent, he chatters with his fingertips; betrayal oozes out of him at every pore."

In contrast to Freud, social psychologist Ross Buck reports on a number of studies that were conducted to identify the ways in which people attempt to disguise or control their emotional responses, often quite successfully. FBI agents, homicide detectives, and professional interrogators who uncover deception for a living reluctantly admit that much of the time, unless the suspect confesses to a crime, they have no idea what the truth is.

For example, consider the recent case of Waneta Hoyt, who claimed that her five children had all died of sudden infant death syndrome over a period of several years. She was able to persuade police that no foul play had been involved by displaying her anguish and grief with convincing tears. Ironically, she had murdered each one of the children because she couldn't stand the sound of their crying, but she used her own tears to direct suspicions elsewhere.

It would seem, then, that tears are among the best indicators of all in signalling internal states, that is, unless the person is unusually skilled in using them for deception. Often, this deception or manipulation can even occur on unconscious levels; the person may not be aware of what he is doing or why. In fact, most of the time each of us gives simplistic reasons to ourselves and others as to why we are crying: "I feel sad" or "I feel happy" or "I feel frustrated," as if life is a multiple-choice test with a single right answer.

In some cases, there are both authentic and contrived components to the display of tears—some of the feeling emanates from inside, while another part resonates in response to the behavior of others. In both cases, crying transcends verbal language; it bypasses that part of our brain that decodes words, and strikes deep into our hearts.

Human Experience Is Defined by Tears

Almost every encounter we have ever had with tears, whether our own or another's, is forever singed into our memories. We cannot think about these tearful episodes, I mean really relive them in our minds, without experiencing sensory flashbacks. Recall, for instance, a recent time in which you shed tears—not a few drops but a full-scale weeping event. It is as if that whole experience is forever preserved symbolically in the crying that took place. If you were so inclined, you could remember the most vivid details about what happened.

The haunting images of past tears form the foundation of all that we are as emotional beings. When we have cried and with whom we have shared these tearful encounters are among the most powerful remembrances we have of intimacy with ourselves and others. These were periods when we were most vulnerable, but also most alive in the intensity with which we were experiencing our feelings. They were times when we truly let ourselves go.

Crying is an experience that comes upon us, rather than something that we just do. It seems to have a force of its own, a will to express itself. Certainly we have some say in the matter—there are times when we do feel like crying, when we can even make ourselves weep with a triggering thought.

If you doubt this, simply bring to mind the vivid image of a time in which you lost someone or something very dear to you. Death. Divorce. Disillusionment. Any major disappointment in your life produced a time for tears, whether you allowed them to flow or not.

For many people, especially those of the male persuasion, crying used to be a natural act, but it was teased out of us by our parents and peers when we were much younger. When we occasionally cannot help ourselves, during those rare moments when the tears come of their own accord, we expend most of our energy trying to stop or at least moderate their flow. We hear a voice in our heads: "You look like an idiot, a simpering wimp, blubbering like that. Get it together!" So, as unobtrusively as possible, you casually wipe a sleeve across your eyes and try to think about something else.

You feel torn, however. In some ways, tearful experiences are magical. They represent those times when you are most moved, when you are most alive, in the sense that your head and your heart, your very spirit, are all synchronized in a single effort to communicate what is going on inside you. You may cry reluctantly, yet feel proud of the times you've let yourself go, as if you have accomplished something meaningful. Tears can symbolize the most genuine part of us—they honor the primacy of our heartfelt emotions. This is particularly the case when the messages we are sending out to others are recognized, acknowledged, and understood.

Tears and Shame
As difficult as it might be to sit with someone who is crying, it is often just as uncomfortable to accept your own tears.

Perhaps you can recall being driven to tears of frustration and indignation by someone who threatened you in some way. There may have been a time when you broke down in tears of outrage, feeling misunderstood and overwhelmed, when someone sat in stony judgment of you. Certainly you can remember crying on behalf of others who were in excruciating pain—you could feel their anguish so intensely it became contagious. You may also have been moved to tears watching a loved one, your eyes literally overflowing with joy for this person for whom you care so much. Most difficult of all have been the times in which you have felt shameful for losing control of yourself, embarrassed by your own tears and the weakness you believe they represent.

At one time, we all knew how to cry quite fluently. When you fell off your bike and hurt yourself, you cried naturally. When your father or mother screamed at you for doing something wrong, you easily burst into tears. Yet now, as adults, about the only time most of us cry is during vicarious experiences in which we are wounded by what is happening to fictitious others in a novel, movie, or television show. We have learned not to cry for ourselves except in the most dire circumstances; even then, it will be a muffled affair.

There are also the embarrassing experiences we have when other people cry. We feel so helpless, so impotent. We want to make everything all right, to do something to stem the flow of tears or turn the faucet off altogether. Those of us who are therapists work even harder to be rescuers. We tried to save our own families as children, and when that failed, we became healers. Even with professional training and lots of practice, we still don't feel comfortable around people who cry. That, you can imagine, is an occupational hazard for a therapist, sort of like a trapeze artist who does not like heights or a fisherman who avoids the water.

You will see in later chapters how shame is programmed by cultural and gender indoctrination, that crying is a behavior often perceived as socially inappropriate and unseemly, a sign of emotional instability or weakness of character. The messages we often get from those around us to stifle our tears are in direct contrast with the physical and emotional needs we feel to express them. It is no wonder that we often feel so ambivalent about our tears.

Crying Occurs in a Context

One of the difficulties inherent in the language of tears is that the same behavior can mean so many different things. It is sometimes not even clear whether a person is really communicating directly to you, or whether the message is really intended as a kind of private, internal memo in which one part of the self is trying to get the attention of another.

Until you can determine the historical, cultural, developmental, and interactive context for tearful behavior, the significance of this communication cannot be reliably derived. Crying has different meanings depending on the person's age, gender, family and cultural background, and especially what transpired to spark the tears.

As a student of tears, you will learn to attend more carefully to the underlying meaning of this behavior by asking yourself a series of questions: If these tears could talk, what would they say? How is the crying adaptive and helpful to the person? Is this communication designed primarily as a private or public statement? How does this behavior fit within the larger context of what I know, sense, observe, and feel?

Wants and Needs

During a tearful outburst you may want the pain to go away, but you may really need to deal with the underlying issues that are being expressed. You may want sympathy from others, but you may really require confrontation in order to work things through constructively. You may want relief, but you may need to be understood.

In the chapter about responding to others' crying, you will learn about translating the language of tears into specific steps you can take to make a difference. Before you offer sympathy or support, compassion or advice, a hug or a good shake, you must first determine what is likely to be most helpful at that moment. This task is made all the more difficult because people don't often know what they are asking for—their language of tears transcends their own conscious awareness of needs. And when they are able to articulate what they want from you, it's not necessarily in their best interest to comply.

During a tearful bout some people respond best to silent holding and listening, others to probes about what is bothering them, still others to vigorous challenges. These rules of engagement are not even consistent for the same person over time. Initially, someone may very well just want to be accepted, but over time that is no longer enough; a more proactive sort of intervention is useful.

For each and every encounter with tears, you will have to help translate the language into messages that are clearly understood, not just by you but by others.

Tears and Intimacy

Until you can make sense of what others are communicating by their tears, you will never experience true closeness with others. Mutual understanding between friends, partners, or lovers can take place only when participants feel free enough to express themselves both intellectually and emotionally. What people want most during bouts of crying is not only help resolving a particular problem but also to be heard and understood. It is through tears that we make contact with others on the most primal level.

One man describes how a breakthrough in a relationship occurred as a direct result of shared tears:

> Like most guys, I guess I don't cry very much. Well, really not at all. It's been years since the last time I really cried. I don't even remember when exactly.
>
> I have this friend whom I've known all my adult life. We went to school together. We would get together for a beer on occasion, swap stories about how great each of us was doing. Yeah, we'd lie a little.
>
> I considered him one of my closest friends and I'm sure he would say the same about me. The weird thing, though, is that we hardly knew one another. I can't say that we were really intimate in any significant way.
>
> It wasn't until he found out he was dying of cancer, with only a few weeks left to live, that we had our first real heart-to-heart talk. We both cried together until our eyes hurt. I hugged him and smelled him and stroked his hair. I told him I loved him and how much I would miss him. But most of all, it was the crying we did together that broke through the restraints in our

relationship. It took impending death to get our attention to the point that we were finally willing to let ourselves go.

The really amazing thing is that since my friend died, one of his gifts to me was helping me to cry again. I find that now I can cry pretty easily. Sometimes, I even want to cry with certain people I trust. It has brought me closer to my dad, some of my friends, and mostly my wife, who really appreciates me being expressive.

Deciphering the Meaning of Your Own Tears

Until you can decode the meaning of your own tears, you will never address the issues in your life that are most significant. If crying occurs during times of greatest vulnerability and emotional arousal, then these episodes represent brief periods of opportunity in which it is possible to deal with your most heartfelt emotions and your deepest core concerns.

Strangely, crying is one of the few emotional displays that functions as more than just a way to communicate to others. After all, there are times when you are prone to cry by yourself, without an audience. Under such circumstances, your tears are not so much a form of communication as much as they are a leaking of internal states of feeling.

According to neurologist Antonio Damasio, the body is a theater for emotions, a stage where feelings are acted out, not just for the benefit of others but for yourself as well. Crying becomes a way that private feelings, some of which may be beyond your awareness, are expressed authentically and spontaneously.

When you listen to the language of your own tears, you are focused on the essence of your life. You are attending to the one part of your existence that combines the physical, emotional, cognitive, and spiritual dimensions.

Each of the points highlighted in this chapter will be elaborated throughout the book, illuminating one of the most intimate and perplexing aspects of your behavior. You have been crying your whole life, and standing by helplessly as others have done the same, without a complete understanding as to what these tears are all about.

In the next chapter, we continue our journey as students of tears by exploring crying as an embellished language system that augments spoken words. It is a particular dialect that is derived from the larger family of languages we recognize as emotional expression. Like smiling, gesturing, posturing, or even bellowing, crying exists primarily to communicate that which can not be said with strictly verbal language. If a picture is worth a thousand words, then a flow of tears can contain a million.

2

a language
that transcends words

I don't want to diminish the magic of tears or minimize the hold they have over us by reducing their meaning in the same way that language teachers made us conjugate verbs or diagram the structure of sentences. Nevertheless, there is some value to looking at this emotional subject with a degree of logical detachment, especially if we are able to connect it to other things that we know something about.

In this chapter we will examine the subject of crying in a larger context, both as a means of communication and within the larger family of emotional expression. Through the voices of several people describing their experiences, we will also review a dictionary of tears, one that lists the principal varieties that you will encounter.

TEARS IN THE FAMILY OF EMOTIONS

Linguists, editors, and other experts on the uses of language are fond of identifying patterns in communication, especially those that provide underlying clues as to what a person means to say. Over time, they have given names to the various parts of speech, like adverbs and adjectives, and have invented labels to describe violations of grammatical rules such as dangling participles and split infinitives.

Tears, as we shall see, also have distinct patterns of communication. Cultural linguists describe crying as a kind of *para*-language that deliberately or unconsciously supports verbal emotional expression. Along with other voice modifiers like drawls, clipped tones, laughter, or even silences, human speech is further articulated by these communication tools, as well as by gestures, postures, and facial expressions. As such, crying is intended as an enhancer of spoken words.

Yet even as a paralanguage, crying has a definite structure with its own process and patterns. Treating crying as a language system, we can describe a set of norms for its use, complete with parts of speech. We can also recognize instances when someone has deviated from conventional norms established by the prevailing standards for her time, culture, gender, and setting.

As in any linguistic investigation in search of patterns, even those that transcend words, we must first understand the larger context from which the particular language evolved. Just as we might study Latin, Greek, or Sanskrit as the basis for understanding contemporary patterns of speech, so too must we delve briefly into the larger perspective of emotional reactions in general as a basis for understanding crying.

I'm following this line of inquiry not only because the study of emotions provides a foundation for understanding the language of tears, but also, quite frankly, because so little has been written about crying. During the process of answering the question posed in the next section, what emotions are for,

I consulted dozens of books on the subject and was surprised to find that crying is usually not even mentioned. It is as if this behavior, one of the greatest mysteries of human experience, is not really a legitimate subject of serious study, at least by those who write books on emotion.

THE CONNECTION BETWEEN
THINKING AND FEELING

Historically, it has been reason, not emotion, that has been most valued by our society. Passionate feelings are usually viewed as dangerous, irrational, and unstable. Only recently have feminist theorists pointed out that as long as patriarchal systems have been in control, masculine values of logic have subjugated feminine ideals of emotional sensitivity. Thus, theologians, philosophers, politicians, and scientists have been rather suspicious of what comes from the heart rather than the head. It is feelings that distract and disorient us, they say, leading us astray from objective truth. Intuition, passion, and emotions are all very amusing, but when there is real work to be done, it is reason upon which we must rely.

But this split between thinking and feeling may no longer be warranted. On the most primal level, visceral reactions like crying are inseparable from both cognitive activity and the neurological mechanisms that drive it. According to neurologist Antonio Damasio, passion and reason are interconnected in a way that enables them to act as internal guides that help us communicate to others what we want and what we need. Feelings, with their corresponding tearful reactions, are not the same as pure emotions, which represent physiological events inside the brain. Rather, feelings are the experiences we have of internal body changes in conjunction with associated mental images. They are the most primary of all sensations, to the body, the mind, and the spirit. "Because the brain is the body's captive audience," Damasio writes, "feelings are winners among equals." They influence our thinking, our subsequent behavior, our very being.

Except for the work of poets, the study of emotions has been initiated primarily by scientists interested in explaining this phenomenon by a typically rational, objective method. Since Charles Darwin's seminal work investigating how animals and humans express themselves emotionally, hundreds of theories have been offered. A half dozen different fields have staked out their territory—sociology, anthropology, linguistics, education, biochemistry, social psychology—each emphasizing different aspects of the phenomenon.

The philosopher William James described emotions as bodily experiences. Sigmund Freud regarded emotion as raw psychic energy in need of discharge. Novelist and philosopher Albert Camus discussed the subject as an extension of his existential beliefs; for him, emotions were the result of the choices we make. More contemporary thinkers have framed emotions as states of physiological arousal, unconscious desires, interactional patterns, imagery, cognitive processes, or linguistic structures.

It is clear from many of these explanations that emotions serve quite a number of purposes. They are certainly a discharge of energy, a state of physiological arousal, but they are also a form of distance regulation in relationships; they draw people closer to us or push them away. They are, in the words of nineteenth-century journalist Ambrose Bierce, the determined effort on the part of the heart to shut down the head.

Most of what has been said about emotional responses in general can be said about the language of tears in particular. Crying is like all other forms of visible emotional arousal in that the body is signaling to others, or to ourselves, that something significant is taking place inside that is hidden from view. Similar to other emotional reactions, crying is ignited within the central nervous system. During sexual arousal, genitals become inflamed. During embarrassment, cheeks become flushed. During anger, voice tone is raised. In a comparable way, tears and weeping are the observable actions that accompany internal states.

Yet crying is also quite unlike any other form of emotional expression in that, as a language, it can be translated so many different ways. Look at a person crying and it could take you a moment to two to tell whether this person is feeling sad or happy or disappointed or relieved or angry, or any one of a dozen other possibilities. People like psychologist Richard Lazarus, biochemist William Frey, or neurologist Simon LeVay, who have spent a lifetime studying emotional reactions like crying, are most perplexed by the phenomenon that tears can result from so many different forms of arousal. Tears can even originate in different parts of the brain—from the limbic system, which controls primary emotions, to the cortex in more reflective bouts of crying.

VOCABULARY OF TEARS

Let's now move from the subject of crying as a language to the specific vocabulary of tears. This vocabulary of crying captures many different feelings all at once, and just like certain words, the same utterance can have a variety of possible meanings. That's why the words come out as tears in the first place—because speech is so inadequate to describe what we are feeling.

As I review some of the types of tears, many of them will be within the realm of your experience, and others will seem quite foreign to you. This is one of the most fascinating aspects of this phenomenon, that so many meanings are possible in a single act. If we were to catalogue the variety of situations in which people are known to weep, we would find a range of examples, each of which carries a different significance. Each of these experiences will be illustrated through the voices of people who may sound very familiar.

Physiological Responses

At the most primary level, tears result from physical responses to bodily stress. These physiological reactions are sparked most obviously by irritating substances (particles of dust, allergies, stray eyelashes) or fumes in the air (onions, ammonia). Acute injuries also will easily trigger tears, both as an expression of unbearable pain and as a cry for sympathy and comfort. After falling down and scraping their knees, children are known to first look around to see who is watching before they let out a bloodcurdling scream. At other times, the pain is so traumatic, tears emerge quite on their own as a statement no less dramatic than blood that leaks out of the wound.

People are also known to cry when there are changes going on within the body rather than the environment. The most obvious example of this occurs at times related to a woman's menstrual cycle, but other common instances when tears are likely to emerge are during hormonal changes, migraine headaches, or other physical ailments. Fatigue is also a culprit, sometimes when it is mixed with emotional reactions.

After a man finished running a marathon race, for example, he described these reactions:

> As I crossed the finish line, tears just started flowing. Yes, I was exhausted, drained, out of my mind, but I also felt so elated and proud. It was as much an emotional as well as physical challenge for me. I cried because I had accomplished something that I had thought was out of reach. I also cried because I just had nothing left in me.

Another example of a tearful physical experience is described by a woman who sometimes finds that a particularly strong orgasm can bring tears to her eyes: "The overwhelming emotion floods my being, leaving me shaken and spent."

Whereas this first entry in our vocabulary of tears involves essentially a physical reaction that is ignited by some intrusion in the present, the next type of crying is related to events in the past.

Reminiscence

It is certainly reasonable to claim that a large amount of crying is related to personal memories. Your consciousness, your sense of self, your very being, is composed of a collection of images, memories, and reminiscences. While some of these images are accurate representations of events that actually took place, many of them are distorted over time. The clarity of details deteriorates over long-term storage. Other memories are altered for your own convenience, to rewrite history in a way that makes it easier for you to live with. Still other events were so painful that they are buried as deeply as possible.

Anything that you encounter in the present connects to your past. Anything that you find disturbing or arousing enough to cry for right now also connects to images and memories in your personal history. Any time you cry for someone else, you are also crying for yourself. In other words, any experience that you have that leads to tears results in part from present circumstances, and yet also results from associations with what you lived in the past. Meaning is constructed through the integration of experience.

Run through a checklist of the most recent times that you have cried. Embedded in the episode will be not only the present stimulus that first sparked the tears but also some remembrance of the past. One man, when asked to make this connection to a recent crying episode, found that sometimes the relationship between events isn't all that obvious:

> At first, I just couldn't see any connection, but I cried when I saw that movie about the Holocaust. Even though I'm not Jewish, and don't really know anyone who was caught up in that whole thing, I still felt horrible for all those people. My tears didn't have anything to do with me—I was just feeling sorry for those survivors who had to live with all that stuff for the rest of their lives.

I kept wondering what on earth this could have to do with me. How was I crying for myself, too? Then I had this immediate picture of walking down the halls in high school and how scared I felt most of the time that these guys would beat me up if I accidently bumped into them.

Upon further reflection, this man realized that although he was crying in response to what had happened in the film, he was also feeling tearful over the bigger picture of terror, of injustice, of being bullied. He was not consciously aware of the source of his tears as they were happening, but after a little thought he was able to draw connections to his own experiences with feeling terrorized. His tears, which at first seemed to be about a movie, were also about his own painful reminiscences.

While it may be taking things a bit too far to claim that all crying is really about memories, there is no doubt that some tearful episodes in our lives are clearly ignited by remnants of the past we would prefer to forget.

A woman in her forties has been struggling to come to terms with the loss and grief of her own childhood. She could shed a lifetime of tears, and yet she feels like she will never cry enough:

I was sitting in the car eating a burrito. I was feeling anxious, not knowing why I was so uneasy. For some reason, I began thinking about being sexually abused by my stepfather. All of a sudden, the burrito changed into a penis. It tasted like sweat and urine. I knew it was a burrito and forced myself to eat it. Chewing hard, symbolically releasing any power it used to have over me.

> I began watching a little girl across the street coming out of her house to talk to her mother. The girl was about the same age that I was when the abuse first began. I watched her in her nightgown, playful and appearing so happy and free. She looked innocent and naive. At that moment, I began to cry over the loss of my own innocence. It felt overwhelming to me that I must have once been that innocent and carefree, but that it was taken away from me.

Even reading these stories can bring tears to our eyes, so poignant and authentic is the pain of the narrators. This is true with respect not only to tears of loss but also to other strong emotional reactions.

Redemption and Release

The therapeutic value of crying is often found in its power to leach out painful memories of the past. If there is one thing that people consistently say about the ways their tears are helpful to them, it is that they are a means of letting go of haunting images. Whereas the previous entry in our dictionary of tears refers to reminiscences that continue to be haunting, this type of tears includes crying that leads to some resolution of past conflicts or some relief in present circumstances.

As a child, Howard never had the opportunity to speak about the anguish he was living on a daily basis—he had been emotionally and physically abused by his parents. It was through his tears rather than through words that he attempted to communicate what he was experiencing, even if nobody else paid much attention. He tried his best to convey to others the extent of his wounds, but his shame stifled his voice:

The church was the only place I felt truly safe as a child. My family did not come with me. As soon as I slid into a pew, my eyes would brim with tears and I would fight them the rest of the hour. But in the serenity and safety of the church, the tears would come. Sliding down my face, causing me to bite my lip and shake my hair around my face to hide them. Did Jesus see me cry? Did no one see me cry? For such a brief time I would expose myself, free myself from the constraints of the game that was imposed on me.

Just as tears offered Howard some release as he suffered abuse in the past, occasional crying in the present allowed him to seek some sort of redemption from circumstances that, while beyond his control, nevertheless elicited feelings of guilt, shame, and humiliation. Tears of release became for him the primary way he attempted to put the past behind him.

In Connection to Others

"For better or worse" goes the phrase in the marriage vows. The same can be said as well for the type of tears that bond us to others. In the best sense of what it means to cry with others, tears are shared during ceremonies that mark transitions that are considered significant in our lives—weddings, funerals, bar mitzvahs, baptisms, baby namings, graduations. Such experiences connect us in ways that could not otherwise be accomplished. It is such a different sort of exchange to cry during an embrace rather than simply shaking hands and offering verbal condolences or congratulations.

In a similar way, tears that accompany departures act as bonding messages that lead to closer intimacy. When children leave home or family members go off on long trips, expressions of love and sadness are expressed most authentically not through our words or gifts but through our tears. You would only have to look around you at any airport to see the powerful, moving ways that people say goodbye to one another when they cry together.

One other variation of this type of tears is associated with human compassion and empathy. People are known to cry when they witness acts of heroism or altruism. In one case, a woman describes crying copiously in response to simply reading a story about a group of teenagers who shaved their heads in a show of unity for one of their friends who lost his hair while undergoing chemotherapy:

> I thought that was so beautiful, I just couldn't help myself. We always hear these stories of the horrible things that people do to one another, and yet here was an instance where a group of kids really showed their love for one another. Reading that story just made me feel so good.

What made this woman feel uplifted was the closer connection she felt to others. Simple acts of kindness trigger in us a reaction of sympathetic empathy in which tears communicate the extent to which we are moved.

Grief and Loss

This is the most acceptable of all types of tears, at least if the crying doesn't go on too long. I have mentioned earlier how crying under circumstances of grief and loss bring people together in a shared experience. As one woman explains, there is a feeling of communal loss:

Crying with others can be like sharing a special meal or wine—it can bond people together as we see one another raw and vulnerable. It is that transparency that holds us together in our common pain and humanity. It is when we feel closest as a family of people.

A second function of tears that represent grief and loss is that they slow down the pace of life so that we have time for reflection. They permit us to honor those we miss, to speak to them and keep them part of our lives:

> Tears come to my eyes when I think of my father who died four years ago of cancer. He was a kind, soft-spoken person. He led a simple life. He was proud of his children, only wanting them to pursue their dreams. It's such a shame that he died without having had the opportunity to achieve his own dreams of seeing the accomplishments of his children and grandchildren. I cry because I miss him terribly. I cry because I feel sorry for myself that he is no longer around.

Tears of loss are experienced in a number of other ways as well, often as a feeling of rejection. In some ways, people feel more devastated by divorce than they do by death. When a loved one dies, people feel sorry for you. You have a right to public mourning. There is nothing personal in all this; you didn't do anything; the loss just happened.

When a relationship ends by the other person's choice, however, there is more than grief. You feel a rejection of your core, as if you are worthless. You feel hopeless. You are struggling not only with the loss of the person you loved, but also with the loss of your esteem and self-respect. It is hardly a clean break as it is with death. You will continue to see this person, hear about him or her, even deal with that person being involved in another relationship. One woman recalls:

> I can remember the day, the hour, and the setting when I was so devastated, in so much emotional pain, that I was barely breathing. My tears were uncontrollable. I was sobbing to the point where I couldn't catch my breath. I was begging my boyfriend not to leave me. He wouldn't listen. He turned and walked away, shutting the door and shutting me out of his life. He left me alone to cry by myself and deal with my broken heart.

> I felt at that moment I would never be the same again, that I would never pull myself together again. He was the center of my life. We planned to spend the rest of our lives together. There has never been a cry since then that has been so devastating. Maybe it was for the best, or so I tell myself.

This is a story of tears that most of us can easily relate to. It has been years, even decades, since these losses occurred, yet they still leave open wounds. We are all haunted by unresolved issues of our past, by lost love, by trauma and tragedy, even by emotional neglect or abuse. We are still crying for these losses; perhaps we always will, until the day we die.

Despair and Depression

With those who are severely depressed, crying is like breathing; it is the way they take in energy, inhaling through ragged sobs of hopelessness rather than gentle breaths of life. They hate their tears, symbols of their helplessness and hopelessness. They feel out of control, as if their bodies have been invaded by an alien spirit, yet it is an all-too-familiar state.

There are few experiences more horrifying then being alone with someone who is hopelessly, suicidally despondent. One such woman, who had not as yet responded to any anti-depressant medication or therapy, could not even complete our interview about her experience.

The whole time she remained mute and immobile. There was a steady stream of tears flowing onto her silk blouse, which couldn't begin to soak up all the excess liquid. I wondered, partially to distance and distract myself from her pain, whether she might not be better off wearing cotton; I was feeling so helpless I almost wanted to suggest that to her as the only constructive thing I could offer. There were wads of tissue overflowing from her hands, spilling onto her lap, a few strays lying by her feet.

She alternated between at least three different stages of tearfulness. First, there was a languid, resting cry with little movement or noise, just her head bowed, hiding her face beneath a cascade of hair. That state would slowly build into deep wracking sobs, occasionally punctuated by wails of "Oh God! Oh God!"

As I watched her nervously (What will I do if she gets worse? Can *anyone* be any worse?), I reflected on what useful purpose these tears were serving. She was drowning in them, going down for the third time.

In a soothing voice, I offered what comfort I could, only to spark still a third stage of tears—a kind of staccato burst of gasps, as if she was strangling. Whatever I said to her (and I tried everything a therapist could think of) had little notice-able effect except to boost the intensity of her despair. Finally, I reconciled myself to the reality that this was the only way she would (could?) speak to me. This was her language and, unfortunately, I could hear her only too clearly—this was someone who was dying from the inside out. Her tears were out of control, and whatever purpose they once served to get some help, the emergency siren was stuck at the on position.

Joyful and Aesthetic Transcendence

Although we often associate crying with anguish, or even with attempts to win sympathy, there is a whole other set of circumstances that provoke tears of joy and rapture. Even though the primary feeling is one of bliss, our being can be so moved as to produce tears, such as the experience described by a new mother:

> It was truly a miracle. All I could do was cry. They were tears of relief, of amazement, of love. With this birth came the realization that my husband and I created this beautiful child—that we could actually make a baby!

Other forms of tearful joy such as aesthetic and spiritual transcendence are similarly elicited by what is perceived as miraculous. One difference, however, is that feelings of exaltation that result from a glorious sunset, a musical passage, or a work of art are all considered by some experts to be an exaggerated appreciation of reality. They represent a distortion of what is really happening in the outside world.

Psychologist Kerry Walters takes issue with the claim by scientists that aesthetic tears are technically incoherent, irrational, and incomprehensible. Is a person truly emotionally disturbed because he cries when he hears a Handel flute sonata or views a painting by Goya? Certainly this is an exaggerated response to a bit of noise or pigment. We know this object is not real, or the image from a musical passage is all in our minds, yet we still experience tearful reactions as genuine, as if we were involved more directly in the movement of action.

In an analysis of the visceral thrills of certain musical passages that can provoke tears in the listener, British psychologist John Sloboda studied the interconnection between sound and psychophysiological responses. He first identified particular musical passages that consistently produce tears, or at least a lump in the throat—excerpts from Rachmaninoff's *Symphony #2,* Beethoven's *Fidelio,* Puccini's *La Bohème,* Bach's *B minor Mass,* Mendelssohn's *Violin Concerto,* or Tchaikovsky's *Romeo and Juliet.* He traced several processes operating in the listeners: the level of intensity of the music, which can't easily be experienced in everyday life; the release of tension after mounting pressure of the imagined story; the associations that are elicited, provoking reminders of losses or reliefs; and anticipated ending of the tension built up by the climactic tones.

In each of these instances, strong emotional responses, including tears, result from the same two types of aesthetic response—feeling moved by the "love theme" in *Romeo and Juliet* because of the vividness with which the story is told, or by the utter perfection of the second piano in Brahms' *Piano Concerto #1.* In all of these cases, Sloboda discovered a whole hidden emotional language embedded in music. Whereas physiological shivers can be elicited most easily through changes in harmonics, and a racing heart by changes in cadence, tears are provoked most reliably by particular changes in melody (called *reductions*) in which the tone one note below is embellished. He cites as the prototypical "tears" passage the opening six bars of Rachmaninoff's *Symphony #2,* 3rd movement, because of its descending harmony.

Music may call forth the most easily studied type of aesthetic or transcendent tears, but far more common are those elicited by spiritual awakenings. Under such circumstances, tears are essentially a private, sacred offering by those who feel moved in their relationship with God. Whereas some religions, such as the Catholic or Mormon Churches, see their institutions as the intermediaries between self and God, a member of the Pentecostal Church attempts to communicate directly with the Higher Power. By speaking in tongues, wailing, and crying, this emotional demonstration is alleged to indicate a true love of God.

In a less ecumenical but hardly diminished context, tears of gratitude can be expressed by anyone as a private offering. Their intent and meaning are not to be viewed by others; in fact, their spiritual significance rests on their solitary prayer. As one man explains:

> There are times when I am driving in my car, mentally reviewing some of the financial pressures I am under—two kids in college, debts piling up, no end in sight. Just when I start feeling overwhelmed, I think about all that I have to be grateful for—my health, the love of my wife, good friends who care about me, and two wonderful children. I just feel so fortunate I want to thank God, so moved sometimes I cry.

This man's tears are not meant to communicate anything, except to himself or to God. In fact, these are the only times in his life when he is moved to tears. When I asked him to describe other times when he cried, he looked at me with a puzzled expression and shrugged.

Solitude can therefore become a special place for tears that are not meant to be revealed. They obviously serve little purpose as a means of communication; they are more an offering. The inside of you is telling the outside of you that something wonderful is going on.

Vicarious Experience

If aesthetically transcendent tears are the ultimate immersion in reality, then this next variety occurs only in an imaginary context. In watching a play, you temporarily suspend your belief during the set changes. During movies or television shows, you agree to imagine that what is happening is real; in fact, it is that willingness to pretend that permits you to cry for joy or weep in sadness over what is happening not to you but to others.

It is interesting to consider why we deliberately *want* to cry. There are movies we go to specifically for that purpose; we even prepare ourselves for the adventure by loading up on tissues ahead of time. We settle down in our seats, encapsulate ourselves in the world on the screen, and then cry on cue whenever the music signals it's time.

Comedy writer David Baddiel is a sucker for these "dambusters." He loves to lose himself in the pathetic, tragic, struggles of the characters, especially love stories between a man and a woman, a boy and an alien, or a woman and a ghost: "It is incredibly exhilarating to feel a sentimental film break through one's heavily encrusted force field of cynicism."

Baddiel is right—we are often too controlled to weep for ourselves. It is far too threatening to confront the tragedies, apprehension, and terrors of our own lives.

Yet, we will enter a darkened room to cry for people we don't know, who are not even real, and pay money for the privilege. We bear no responsibility for their misfortune, as we do for our own losses. We are free to cry precisely because it is not real. It is safe to let ourselves feel because we will not be the ones who are actually hurt. After Baddiel leaves the theater, he says, "I can feel myself holding on hard to the memory of it, trying to prolong the emotions it has aroused, trying to use them to enhance some sense of wonder at the world outside. This can be tough: it's such stuff as dreams are made of, after all, and it doesn't take much to burst the bubble of serenity within which the film has enfolded me."

The pure pleasure of seeing a movie that makes us cry, or frightens the heck out of us, is that we can experience our emotions without personal risk. We have paid mercenaries to fight monsters or risk rejection on our behalf. We can live vicariously on an emotional roller coaster as we laugh one minute, cry the next, experience the thrills of emotional arousal, but get off the ride at the end without even a single hair out of place.

Anger and Frustration

This one has been saved for last because some experts doubt that tears of anger actually exist. Among them, two counselor educators in England, Kingsley Mills and A. D. Wooster, cite examples of when a boy breaks into tears as he is about to fight, or a girl when she has defeated an opponent in an argument. In both of these instances, their crying *looks* like pure anger, but it is really diluted with expressions of fear and apprehension, in which force and energy are directed outward. Yet, a "tearful state is one of blurred vision and a hopeless attitude which matches feelings of discouragement and fear rather than anger."

Whether people are actually angry or not *when* they cry (as opposed to afterward), some report such a feeling in strong doses:

> It was after I got back to my office that I wanted to punch a hole through the son-of-a-bitch's face. I had to stand there and take this abuse . . . from an asshole who doesn't know half as much as I do about the situation. I nodded my head, agreeing with him, seething inside all the while.

> I just lost it as soon as I closed the door. Yes, I was frustrated. Mortified, too. Most of all, though, I was just so angry—at him for the insensitive way he treated me, and at myself for taking it. I felt better after I cried. It was strange, because I actually felt terrible that I let him get to me like this. But I hated myself so much for being that way that I resolved I wouldn't let it happen again.

Although this is an example in which the tears of anger were worked through to a point of resolution, often the emotional overload is turned inward as a form of self-loathing. One of the gender differences we will explore in a later chapter is that women are more likely than men to cry when they are angry or frustrated, having been socialized to restrain aggression. Quite a number of women talk about the link between anger, fear, and crying. Some gender psychologists, led by June Crawford, have noted that anger is essentially an expression of powerlessness; those with real power don't need to be angry.

Crying is often the way that women and girls express their anger, emerging out of a feeling of powerlessness. Primary anger can also be expressed indirectly as secondary hurt. Tears can be used as a punishment, a weapon to fight back against someone who has hurt you. One woman, for example, felt angry that her husband was late from work and didn't call. Since this feeling was unacceptable to her, instead she cried tears of disappointment, sadness, and hurt:

> I started to whimper a little at first, then I heard him come in. The tears started pouring down when I first heard his voice calling out, "Honey, I'm home." I felt empty inside. I felt he had let me down. I had a rotten day and he was out enjoying himself. It wasn't fair.

> He reacted to me in a very consoling manner. He wanted to talk about what my tears were all about, but I just withdrew from him. He laid down beside me and held me in his arms, promising it wouldn't happen again.

Although this woman was not deliberately using her tears to be manipulative, they did have the desired effect of punishing her husband in such a way that he would feel remorseful. There are other instances when crying is used more intentionally as a weapon.

THE SPECIAL VOCABULARY OF MANIPULATIVE TEARS

Our discussion would hardly be complete without considering the role that motivation plays. Although I have mostly been speaking of crying as a heartfelt act, one in which a person spontaneously erupts in response to some tragic or joyful event, it can also be triggered quite deliberately.

If the goal is to win sympathy, elicit guilt, engage in emotional blackmail, bring someone closer or push him away, there are few more effective means than a good cry. As one woman explains:

> Yes, I have been known to get what I want with a few tears. Hey, it's a man's world. They have all the advantages. I use whatever weapons I can.

> I know I got a promotion at work precisely because my boss didn't want to have to deal with my dramatic disappointment in his office. I can put on quite a show when I want to.

> The same with my boyfriend. Say he wants to do one thing and I want to do something else. There is nothing like a tear or two to make my point. He backs down immediately.

As babies, we learned how powerful crying can be to get others to do our bidding. Watch the interactions between a year-old toddler and her parents who are about to leave for the evening. Soon after the baby-sitter takes the child in her arms, the parents head toward the door, only to hear immediate squalls of outrage. Baby has other plans for her parents; she would much prefer they stay at home to keep her company. Once the parents turn back toward her, she stops crying as abruptly as if they had pushed a button. They cuddle her for a minute, offer reassuring words that she can't understand, then turn toward the door once again. Cries begin anew.

This baby, as pediatrician Katherine Karlsrud observes, is learning an important lesson: "Crying and carrying on enable one to gain control over others and achieve instant gratification."

It may very well be that different parts of the brain, different neural pathways, even different muscles are involved in producing genuine as opposed to contrived tears. That astute observer of human and animal behavior, Charles Darwin, noted more than a hundred years ago the differences between a spontaneous and polite smile. The former, involuntary reaction combines the contractions of two muscles, one of which, the *orbicularis oculi,* cannot be controlled through an act of will. In a contrived smile, however, only the *zygomatic major* muscle is mobilized, a much more malleable organ that will do whatever bidding we ask of it.

In the case of crying, as well, just as we will see later how emotional versus onion tears differ in their chemical composition, so too can we assume that spontaneous tears originate in one part of the brain while manufactured tears necessitate greater mental imagery of the cortex, as any method actor can attest.

Satirist Doug Marlette writes about how emotional expression in general, and tears in particular, are used by even sociopaths and perverts to win sympathy and hide from responsibility. He describes how all a child molester or convicted murderer has to do on talk shows is cry on cue to win audience sympathy. Crying can be a cheap trick to get others to feel sorry for us.

If this sounds unduly cynical, consider that most skilled actors can cry on demand, three, four, five takes in a row. Many of them use a technique that works quite well for anyone— just think of your own past, and revisit a tragic time.

We are so impressed with tears, by the way, that a stellar crying performance can influence an Academy Award nomination. In one analysis of Oscar nominees in the categories of Best Actor and Best Supporting Actor, Jim Gullo looked at some of the spoils of weeping during the past few years. Although it isn't completely fair to say that crying was the only component of an Oscar-winning performance, such tearful displays do play a major role in showcasing extraordinary talent. Recall some of these tearful monologues that were so effective that they may even have made *you* cry:

- In 1978, Jon Voight won Best Actor for his tearful speech in *Coming Home*. With a crying style best characterized as "trembling," he showed wet eyes but dry cheeks.
- Two years later, Robert DeNiro captured the same award for his blubbering, incoherent sobs after throwing a fight in *Raging Bull*.
- That same year, it was a sweep for tearful performances. Timothy Hutten cried passionately, unabashedly, in *Ordinary People* as he recounted the death of his brother. A Best Supporting Actor Award resulted.
- In 1985, Jack Nicholson in *Prizzi's Honor* and William Hurt in *Kiss of the Spider Woman* cleaned up at the Oscars for their melodramatic but restrained weeping.
- For one of the few times in movie history, Tom Hanks won an Oscar in 1994 for shedding tears of joy. In *Philadelphia,* playing a dying AIDS victim, he cried while appreciating the perfect beauty of an aria by Maria Callas.

The trend continues to this day. Crying by men and women moves us like no other expressive gesture. If professional actors can pretend to cry so well that they literally win Academy Awards, just imagine people who are far more unscrupulous using tears to garner support, win sympathy, influence outcomes, and manipulate others.

Another and far more common use of tears as an agent of manipulation is described by one woman:

> Sure, I can cry when I want to, but I don't waste tears unless I really, really need them. The other day I was at a department store trying to return a pair of shoes that the manager said had been worn too much to take back.
>
> I pleaded. I begged. I threatened to not return. Then I cried. Sort of a pitiful, helpless kind of cry. It was not my best performance, but it did the job. He took the shoes back. And apologized!

In defense against accusations that such tears are unduly melodramatic, if not manipulative, the woman replied: "Women cry because it is the only way their feelings will be validated."

For both sexes, crying is indeed a language that transcends words, a way of communicating with its own special rules of grammar and its own unique vocabulary. In later chapters, we will look much deeper at gender differences in the ways people understand and speak specialized vocabularies of crying.

In the next chapter, we'll explore the mechanisms by which crying evolved to play such an important role in the expression of feeling. How is it that crying developed as a communication and signal system only among our species? What functions have tears been designed to serve? How do they operate adaptively to help us get what we want?

3

evolution of crying

T ears began their lives more than a million years ago as an eye-cleansing system for the human cornea, a kind of windshield washer that automatically turns itself on in response to irritants in the air. Only in *Homo sapiens* did this eye water also evolve as part of an intricate system of language in which complex feelings could be expressed in capsulated form.

We humans are unique, but it is not the use of fire nor the opposable thumb that distinguishes us from other creatures. According to neurophysiologist Paul MacLean, who studies the evolution of the brain as an organ of emotion, it is the ability to cry tears in response to separation from loved ones that sets us apart. He presents an intriguing theory that crying tears in humans first began about 1.4 million years ago when the use of fire first came into common use. He hypothesized that the accompanying smoke first sparked tearing reflexes. MacLean reasons that as tribespeople sat around fires to cook, cauterize wounds, bid farewell to family members, and dispose of loved ones in cremation ceremonies, tearing became a conditioned reflex associated with separation.

Whether this provocative hypothesis is based in reality

or not, it does draw attention to the bonding nature of tears that are part of so many of our rituals. Regardless of whether this behavior developed as a conditioned reflex or, just as likely, evolved through natural selection because of its other functional uses in communication and interaction, it is clear that especially among infants, fluent criers get their needs met more readily than those who don't make a peep.

EVOLUTIONARY FUNCTIONS OF TEARS

It is ironic that Charles Darwin, the master of evolutionary adaption, considered tears to be an exception to his rule that all behavior is naturally selected based on its adaptive value in helping an organism survive—he could find no useful purpose served by tears; he speculated that they were simply the insignificant accompaniment to engorged blood vessels and contracted muscles surrounding the eyes. He was sorely puzzled, evolutionarily speaking, by how this behavior could possibly contribute to the survival of an individual. This senseless noise didn't seem to contribute in any way to the likelihood of survival and procreation.

There are, in fact, many very important reasons why crying has evolved from its original purpose of producing an antiseptic fluid to keep the eyes free of bacteria and foreign particles. The fittest for survival also include those who are most skilled at direct and indirect means to get their needs met. Since so much of human interaction revolves around reciprocal favors, asking for help through direct verbal request involves one level of payback; it is understood that at some future time you will respond with as much, or perhaps even more, investment of time, energy, and resources. If, however, you can solicit help indirectly, through the plea of tears, for example, then the expectation of reciprocal rewards would be somewhat less. After all, you didn't actually ask for help, even though you appreciate that it was offered. Successful people—meaning, in evolutionary terms, those who live long, productive lives and are able to produce multiple offspring—tend to be those who have both assertive and subtle options for soliciting help from others even when they are not initially disposed to offer it.

In acquiring any of the strategies to help us survive, we have, just like all animals, certain reflexes (eye blinks, pupil dilation, startle responses), instincts that are driven by hormones (sex), and drives (hunger, thirst). Yet humans are unique in their survival as a species in that it takes us an extraordinarily long time to launch a child into the world. Once our ancestors learned to walk upright, changing forever the shape of a mother's birth canal, and once our brains evolved to be so large that our heads would not pass through the opening if the brain was fully developed, Nature designed a plan whereby we were evicted from the womb as unfinished business. Whereas many animals can get around quite well even a few hours after their birth, human young need several years to complete their development before they can fend for themselves. This means they need some way to keep adults motivated and patient enough to stick around long enough to provide food, shelter, and protection against predators.

All emotional responses, and the means by which to

elicit them in others, evolved as a way to increase attachment bonds between infants and parents. In spite of all species' biological urge to care for their offspring, some fish eat their young, and most land animal parents stick around for only a few seasons. However, emotions sink deep roots into human hearts, motivating us to invest ten, even twenty years or longer, until our children can take care of themselves.

Once survival of the fittest is expanded to include not only those who are the strongest, swiftest, and smartest, but also those who are most emotionally sensitive and expressive to augment their ability to communicate, we can see how such behavioral characteristics would stick around over time as somewhat useful. Those who have developed high levels of emotional receptivity are likely to be more successful in their interactions with others. Historically, such individuals survived at a greater rate than those who didn't master the intricacies of emotional signals. Since they produced more offspring, our species has evolved greater emotional sensitivity (and tears) over time—through natural selection.

It is not just the ability to cry that is considered adaptive—but to cry *well,* in such a way that it invites help rather than retribution. Looking at the crying behavior of infants, for example, pediatrician Ronald Barr spoke of the paradoxical nature of crying as both highly adaptive and dysfunctional. When babies cry effectively, they get their needs met—their diapers changed and food delivered to their cribs. Interestingly, crying even stimulates milk production in the mother, so it actually acts to produce more nourishment. Yet, if taken too far, excessive crying leads to parental frustration—in some cases, even to child abuse. More than a few parents who have murdered their children explained with a helpless shrug: "He just wouldn't stop crying."

So, being able to cry frequently or loudly is not a good predictor of effective survival by itself; you must also be able to time your outbursts according to the tolerances of those around you. Further, you must be able to cry in a way that your language is understood.

Since tears are the only language available to babies, we certainly don't have the option of asking them to elaborate on what they mean: "Excuse me, baby, but does this cry mean you are hungry, or just fussing for a little while to work off some excess energy?"

Sound spectrographs have been used to analyze the most detailed features of crying behavior in infants. Pediatric acoustic diagnosticians Howard Golub and Michael Corwin report on various features in evidence, some with the most interesting descriptive names. In addition to simple duration, pauses, and pitch of the cry, investigators examine melody (rising and falling), harmonics (frequencies), furcations (split signals evident in pathological cries), and glottal plosives (release of pressure), just as they would in a piece of music.

With such data available, skilled diagnosticians can determine from the acoustic features of a cry whether there is brain damage from oxygen deficiency at birth, jaundice (a strong cry suddenly breaks into weaker ones), hypothyroidism (oscillating vibrato), or respiratory distress (double harmonics). There are fascinating clues available in a simple cry for those who are sensitive enough to hear them.

Crying was originally designed as short bursts announcing distress. Not only was this easier on the ears, it was also less likely to attract enemies or predators. So, prolonged crying in infants, as in the case of colicky babies, is a relatively recent phenomenon in our evolution. Barr believes this strategy evolved as a way for the baby to discourage the mother from producing another sibling for a while. As long as the parents have their hands full with their current child, they won't create more competition for food and resources. While a largely speculative theory, such thinking does provide at least one possibility to account for why such apparently dysfunctional crying as occurs in colicky babies has continued to persist.

The Signal System in Newborns

There are three primary infantile signals that are with us from the earliest age that are designed to bring adult care: crying, smiling, and laughing. Whereas the first signal is switched off by this attention, the latter two are switched on by it. In other words, crying is what brings the parent to see what the problem is; smiling and laughter are designed to keep the parent around. These three emotional expressions thus evolved as the only way that the infant can get her needs met. As the child becomes more proficient in cooing and smiling, crying as the primary form of emotional expression slowly diminishes in frequency.

On the one hand, we are born with the quite natural tendency to express our feelings, yet on the other hand these displays can be messy, or at least distracting to others. Imagine what life would be like if everyone was crying, screaming, expressing rage, disappointment, or jubilation every time they felt like it. Feelings are thus carefully regulated by sanctions installed to keep us in reasonable control. One of the most obvious places you will see this training take place is on an airplane, when parents are doing their best to stop babies from crying because the setting is considered socially inappropriate.

Strong signals are being sent early in childhood that there are other ways to ask for what you want. In several studies of infant-mother interaction patterns conducted by child psychologists Carol Malatesta and Jeannette Haviland, it was found that an average of eight such signals are sent by mothers to their infants every minute, training them when and how to express their feelings according to expected norms.

Parent-Child Relations

The whole nature of parent-child interaction patterns is first developed around issues related to crying. Depending on how we respond to a child's earliest tears, we begin to formulate the ways that our relationship will be organized. Compare, for example, three different ways that a mother might respond to the identical crying episode that wakes her up at 3 A.M., approximately one hour after the last feeding of her three-month-old infant.

The first mother sprints out of bed, races to the crib side, and immediately attempts to soothe the baby back to sleep. When that doesn't work, she takes the baby back to her bed and holds him until he falls back to sleep.

The second mother waits a few minutes after the crying begins, then ventures a peek into the crib to see how the baby is doing. She speaks softly and reassuringly but decides to leave the baby in place to work things out for himself.

The third mother chooses to ignore the outburst. She knows that her baby is neither hungry nor wet since she had just taken care of those needs an hour earlier. She doesn't wish to reinforce this kind of crying with attention, so she decides to wait things out. After a very long forty-five minutes, finally the crying winds down to whimpers, and then quiet once again.

Each of these three responses to tears is a perfectly legitimate parenting style that reflects both the attitudes of the mother and the very beginnings of the relationship that is developing with her child. These are all *good* mothers, in the sense that experts could agree that any one of these interventions might be best in that situation. The point, however, is that each of these mothers is communicating with her baby in a slightly different way. They all hear the distress call, but they each respond according to their individual interpersonal style. We might visit these same mothers a decade later and very well recognize the same pattern of interaction that first evolved beside the crib.

Look around you at any playground or grocery store and you will observe similar variations in how parents respond to the crying of their children. Two elementary-school-age children, for example, are taking turns jumping off a climbing tower. By accident, one lands on the other, causing each of the children to let out a dramatic wail. One mother immediately rushes over to offer comfort, picks up her child and carries him over to the bench where she had been sitting. He continues to whimper for quite a few minutes while being held and rocked by his parent, reassured that he will be okay.

The other child glances over at his mother, who is watching very carefully to see if he is in fact injured—which he is clearly not. She speaks to him in a clear voice: "You're all right, honey. Just brush yourself off and climb back on." This mother *wanted* to rush over as quickly as the other one, but she chose to communicate a different message to her child in response to his tears: "I am here if you really need me but I think you can work this one out for yourself."

Crying and Temperament

This evolution of crying communication results not only from early parental training in the crib and playground but also from basic physiological differences in organisms. Some people cry more than others because they feel things more intensely. Their nervous systems are calibrated to a higher level of sensitivity in some dimensions. They are more easily aroused, both internally in terms of their cortical activity, endocrine system, and somato-visceral changes, and externally in the ways they express reactions.

Although some of these differences are the effects of learning and socialization, as well as of individual cognitive styles, genetics also plays a role. Babies are born with different temperaments; some are placid, others become distressed very easily.

In a longitudinal study of crying and emotional patterns, developmental researchers Nathan Fox and Susan Calkins found that infants who would cry when a pacifier was removed at two days would also cry easily when they were restrained at five months. Interestingly, however, this emotional sensitivity served them well later in life. When compared to children who had not been easily distressed as infants, early criers were much more adaptive as they grew older. They were more sociable and less disturbed in reaction to normal situations that cropped up. They were also highly skilled at asking for what they wanted in ways other than through their tears.

Whereas crying does serve the purpose of allowing babies to ask for help when they need it, it also has evolved over time to function in a number of other useful ways. At its most basic level, the actions of crying help to keep infants' physiological systems tuned to peak levels, much like revving the engine of a car sometimes helps it to settle into a gentle idle.

BIOLOGICAL FUNCTIONS OF CRYING

Each one of us was prepared to be a perfect crier, to whimper, wail, scream, and shed tears whenever the spirit moved us. In fact, there have been reports by obstetricians indicating that some of us have even been known to cry in the womb!

The birth cry, the most dramatic moment in human life, exists for a number of reasons. Foremost, it is an expression of pain and shock after being subjected to such torture as being squeezed through an impossibly tight tunnel. It is an exclamation of indignation at being pushed out from a warm, quiet, dark, watery place, into one filled with noise, cold, and light. No longer can we float contentedly, taking nourishment through the tube in our bellies, kicking the landlady whenever we prefer to change positions.

The birth cry is thus an exclamation of hunger, shock, and discomfort, but also perhaps of anger and fear. This first cry is also used as a tune-up for breathing and heart function in a new environment. It calibrates our lungs, preparing them to take in air instead of water. Crying is, therefore, the very first thing we do in this life. It is caused by the most basic will to survive.

Crying remains the infant's main form of exercise. It is the highest state of arousal, a kind of limbering of the nervous system, a physiological adjustment process. It generates heat for warmth, increases lung capacity, burns off excess energy, increases mental alertness, and discharges tension. It represents a testing and strengthening of all the equipment that is needed to form language. In order to cry, one has to coordinate respiration, intonation, air pressure, phonics, and muscular control. It is necessary to master the intricacies of the esophagus, larynx, and the abdomen. Once this is understood, it can be seen that crying is part of the body's system of self-regulation—babies cry even though they don't want anything except a little exercise.

As far as the tears themselves, their production helps to immunize the whole respiratory system against infection, since they lubricate mucous membranes in the nose and throat with antibacterial secretions. This process led some early researchers to conclude that this was, in fact, the main purpose of tears: to soothe mucous membranes that would otherwise dry out during the intake and expulsion of sobbing. This theory has since been refuted by others on the grounds that most crying (vocalization) episodes do not necessarily include sobbing (irregular breathing). In addition, there are other times we breathe rapidly, such as during vigorous exercise, yet we don't need to cry under these conditions.

These observations about the biological basis of crying

have led scientists to study the role of crying in a person's early existence. Until fairly recently, however, relatively little was known about some of the biochemical differences among the various kinds of tears, which appear to serve different purposes altogether.

Biological Differences in Tears

In a modest laboratory tucked away in an obscure corner of a medical complex in St. Paul, Minnesota, a biochemist methodically fed onions into a blender. Bill Frey was concocting the perfect mix of fumes designed to elicit tears on command in his attempts to differentiate physiologically reactive excretions from those that emerge during times of sadness or excitement.

More than a decade ago, Frey conducted the first landmark research on the chemical composition of emotional tears. He was able to isolate prolactin, a hormone also residing in the mammary glands and responsible for milk production, as present in emotional tears. Associated with stress during danger or arousal, prolactin is released by the pituitary gland at times of emotional intensity and finds its way into the lacrimal glands. It appears, then, that some crying may very well be a crucial means by which the body rids itself of substances like prolactin that could become toxic during times of emotional difficulty. Just as the most basic form of tears act as physical cleansers to keep the surface of the eye free of obstructions, this other type of emotional tears may function to clear the body of certain chemicals that build up during stress.

Even though all tears look the same and seem to originate from the same place, they actually are different in their chemical compositions and points of origin in the brain.

Basically there are three biological types of tears, each variety with a different function.

Continuous tears are part of an automatic washing device in the eye that keeps the surface moist and clean. These tears are glandular lubricating fluid, not unlike the oil in your car engine that keeps the working parts functioning smoothly. They operate continuously; every time you blink, your eyelids draw a small amount of fluid to spread evenly over the surface. These tears act largely as a prevention against future problems and even have antibiotic properties to keep bacteria and viruses at bay.

Irritant tears are called into play only during such times when eyes are in danger of damage from external chemicals, objects, or gasses. If smoke, an eyelash, or sulfuric acid emanating from onions comes into contact with your eyes, a flush system is activated to dilute the irritant, eventually washing it away.

Emotional tears represent the uniquely human expression of intense feeling. Not only did Bill Frey and others discover that these tears have higher concentrations of proteins, but the lacrimal glands may also work to excrete chemicals that build up in the body during stress. While little is understood about exactly how this mechanism works, it appears as if the presence of prolactin in the system may make tears flow more fluently. In other words, it may lower the threshold at which crying may begin, and it may act as a control device to keep the tears flowing.

To support his theory, Frey cited research in which a drug, Levodopa, was administered to people who were pathological criers, meaning that they shed tears that were not in response to anything going on around them. Usually the victims of closed head injuries, strokes, or some other organic condition, such patients reduced their crying when given this drug, which is known to reduce prolactin secretions in the pituitary gland. While not definitive evidence to support a theory that is only now being studied at greater length, we can safely say that emotional tears do have distinct chemical properties, suggesting that they serve a much different biological function than the other tears mentioned.

Emotional tears are also controlled by a different region of the brain. If the cranial nerves that control continuous and irritant tears were severed, or if your whole eye was anesthetized, you would still be able to cry emotional tears.

Tears and Health

Similar to other body mechanisms that excrete waste products through urination, defecation, perspiration, and exhalation, emotional tears are a way to remove harmful materials. Manganese, for example, is found to be twenty to thirty times more highly concentrated in emotional tears than in the blood. Even without the built-in filters of the kidney, it seems as if lacrimal glands leach out of the system excessive amounts of this chemical. This may very well mean that people who cry more have a higher need to excrete certain substances. Just as interesting, it may also be that people who stop themselves from crying may be interfering with the body's natural means of waste disposal.

Just as you would experience tremendous discomfort if you didn't go to the toilet when you needed to, inhibiting tear production may also be detrimental to healthy functioning.

Somatic complaints such as sleep disorders and nervous ailments are not uncommon under circumstances of chronic emotional restriction.

It has been said by medical and psychological experts for years that holding in your emotions is not good for you physically. Inhibiting tears was thus said to be associated with hives, ulcers, asthma, colitis, high blood pressure, cancer, and a host of other diseases. To confirm this assumption, Margaret Crepeau studied the crying behavior of adults. She found that people who cry more often and have positive attitudes toward crying are healthier emotionally and physically than those who don't cry or who view it with disdain. She detected similar physiological benefits to laughter. In both cases, blood pressure is lowered, oxygen flow to the brain is increased, and there is a subjective sense of tension release.

While this is an appealing model, some research has not completely supported this claim. In one review of this literature, it was found that people who cry a lot are not necessarily more in touch with their feelings, nor are they more immune to physical illness. If anything, the opposite is true: people who cry frequently are more subject to physical problems throughout their lives and more prone to depression. In another study, James Gross and two other psychologists found that people who cried spontaneously ended up feeling worse than those who didn't, at least in the short run.

Of course, one explanation for this phenomenon is that people who don't cry just don't get upset. "That's the problem," biochemist Bill Frey explains. "People are aroused and distressed during crying. They are upset because they are moved by what they are seeing or living. Crying represents an engagement with life."

Drawing some conclusions from these studies, there seem to be distinctly different ways that people cry. First, there are the tears we associate with the release of tension; it is clear afterward that you feel much better, even if initially you become more upset. People who cry fluently in response to external triggers such as interpersonal conflicts, disappointments, and losses may very well be demonstrating healthy behavior on a par with any other means of stress reduction.

Other kinds of crying may not be in your best interest, especially those that seem related to underlying organic depression that requires chemical intervention with drugs like Prozac in order to stabilize moods.

It is important to keep in mind that there are wide-ranging differences in the ways each of us is constructed, physiologically speaking. The anatomy of your lacrimal glands, the characteristic functioning of your endocrine or neurological systems, are just a few systems that determine crying frequency and intensity. Each of us has a different biological threshold for tears.

To illustrate this point: A fire retardant sprinkler system can be set to go off in response to a major combustion or the smallest wisp of smoke. Likewise, each of us came into the world with a programmed emotional system that was set to go off according to our individual tolerances for smoke and combustion. Through learning, adaptation, experience, socialization, and determined effort, each of us has moved the original settings for our eyes' sprinkler system. In some cases, this recalibration is not functioning in our best interest. During times when we yearn for tranquility, false alarms are set off, causing crying when there is only the illusion of fire. For other people, the heat could be strong enough to vaporize anything within minutes, but there is not a drop of moisture to douse the flames.

Only you can be the judge of whether you are crying too little or too much (of course, you might want to consult with others who know you best). For most people in most circumstances, holding in tears goes against the most natural of inclinations. Although everyone is born knowing how to cry, over time some people lose the capacity for shedding tears. One of the prices that is often paid for this emotional constipation is diminished attachment to others and intimacy in relationships.

TEARS FOR COMMUNICATION AND SURVIVAL

Among all forms of communication, emotional responses are most easily expressed and decoded nonverbally. In less than a second you can glance at a person's face and know intuitively what he is expressing. Furrowed eyebrows, pursed lips, ripples in the forehead, chin resting on hand, and you think "she's confused"—this person seems perplexed by something. Reddened cheeks, tight muscles in the neck and cheeks, smoldering, intense eyes, and the person appears angry to you. Slumped posture, downturned lips, moisture seeping from the eyes, and you instantly recognize sadness. So it goes with a dozen different emotional reactions, each of them recognizable by their visual cues, each of them evolved over time to increase the communication and survival capabilities of our species.

Nature has graciously provided us with signals to help us interpret emotional responses. For example, the raised eyebrows that accompany surprise or interest also represent a widening of the eyes in primates. This physiological adjustment increases visual acuity, thus enabling the person to perceive danger better. Yet the eyebrow raise is a signal to others as well. In fact, the very purpose of the hair above our eyes is to highlight this area so it is easier to communicate interest in one another. More than any other animal, humans stare intently at one another's faces during communication, primarily to observe nonverbal communication that accents the spoken words.

We master the ability to express and read emotion very early in life. By age two, a child already knows how to make a happy or sad face, and just one year later she can tell you what she is feeling. It is also common that in response to a mommy or daddy who is crying—or even pretending to cry—a three-year-old will know to offer comfort. Although there is some debate as to whether this is the result of natural empathy or learned behavior, there is little doubt that humans develop powers of emotional expression and sensitivity at a very early age.

Tears as White Flags

Throughout the animal kingdom there have evolved ways that one individual can signal to others, "I've had enough!" Displays of surrender are part of ritualized combat among almost every species. Among chickens, baboons, or bison, social order is established through a hierarchy of power that results from tests of dominance. Since the only task is to determine who is most qualified to lead, it would not be helpful for members of herds or packs to be killing each other off during challenges. Even if the weakest members were weeded out, it would be at the expense of mortal wounds to the strongest. Instead, there is a way to "cry uncle" and stop the fight before things get out of hand.

When a chimpanzee realizes that he is on the losing end of a fight, he will present his hindquarters as an act of submission. Among other species a white flag of surrender is displayed through withdrawal, passivity, or evidence of subservience. Consider now the similar role that tears play among our kind when someone who is being overly aggressive can be made to back off.

Describing one representative incident of this phenomenon, a man is still stunned months later at the power tears have to abruptly change the way an interaction is going. He describes the circumstances as they unfolded:

> I saw this male physician ripping into a woman administrator at the hospital, really hurting her. He was completely berating her. The rest of us who were standing around watching this spectacle could clearly see that this woman was becoming more and more upset. This doctor, though, wasn't paying any attention. He just kept going on and on with his tirade.

> All of a sudden, a tear welled up in her eye, just a single tear, and ran down her cheek. He stopped cold. This guy, big time surgeon and all, used to having his way and blustering onward,

just stopped dead. This tiny spot of wetness communicated to him very clearly what he otherwise had not seen.

He started backpedaling so fast, apologizing like crazy. That single tear had meaning for him in a way that nothing else did.

What words cannot say, tears can communicate with powerful force.

Drawing People In

Over centuries of evolution we have become more efficient, more focused, in the ways we communicate feeling. Animals read each other by noting posture, gestures, expression, vocalizations, and behavior. A herd of kob will stand calmly near a resting lion, somehow able to read subtle cues that they're not on the menu at the moment.

Mistakes in reading such indicators of internal states can be very costly, not just for a kob who misinterprets a lion's appetite. Imagine approaching a person who sits pensively, chin resting in her palm, shoulders slumped in apparent concentration. Add a single tear to a cheek and you have quite another situation, which requires a different form of approach.

The functions of all emotional displays such as crying are embedded in social contexts. They evolved primarily as a parallel language system that is considerably more sophisticated in its grammar and syntax than any spoken tongue. They inform others about what you are experiencing inside that they could not know in any other way.

But infants aren't the only ones who need strategies by which to "seduce" people into helping them. Some types of crying in adults also work to establish contact by drawing people closer to you, playing on their heartstrings, appealing to their empathy and compassion. This kind of weeping invites people to reach out to you in ways that they would not ordinarily extend themselves.

Imagine, for example, that you are walking down the street and you see someone sitting on a bench, looking forlorn, staring off into space. While disturbed by this scene, you would probably continue on your way. Now imagine a similar scene, but this time the person is cradling herself in her arms, sobs are shaking her body, and tears are streaming down her face. In this second case, you are far more likely to stop and offer assistance than you would in the other instance. This second woman is drawing you in to help her far more effectively than mere expressions of despondency without tears.

Breaking Off Contact

It is amazing enough to consider how well crying works to bring people closer to you; equally impressive is how effective a strategy it is to get people to leave you alone during those times when you wish to close yourself down. This need occurs during times when you want to protect yourself while healing takes place away from the scrutiny of others. After all, tears tend to flow when you are feeling upset, out of control, and not at your best.

Quite a number of similar behaviors that place us in a position of vulnerability have also become associated with the need for privacy. In almost all cultures, for example, excretory functions are shielded from others' view, not just for hygienic purposes but because you are temporarily immobilized. Even the polite ritual of covering a sneeze or yawn with your hands has evolved for reasons other than merely preventing an inadvertent spray. During such times your eyes are closed, and for a second or two you are vulnerable. The hand acts as a temporary shield, as if to say, "Hold everything," and then, "Okay, now I'm with you again."

Of all such behaviors, crying is a time when you are absolutely most vulnerable. Sometimes it feels like a stake has been driven through your heart. It would therefore make sense that you would want some privacy to regain your composure. It would also be logical to assume that tears serve a valuable purpose in sending a clear message to those around you: "Keep away from me right now!"

Tears have thus evolved as a distance regulator that maintains appropriate space. It is an early warning system, like the rattle of a snake trying to protect itself. It provides quick, economical, condensed information to yourself, and others, about your reactions to what is taking place. It buys you some time to process what is happening within you before you attempt to deal with others.

THE EVOLUTION OF UNDERSTANDING

We can speak of evolution in the sense of genetic development, or we can apply this term as well to the process by which people try to make themselves understood. The language of tears is but one of several dialects that we employ when we are trying to communicate messages on an emotional level. This is one of the strongest drives that we feel in contemporary life—the motive to connect to others.

The history, biology, and development of crying as the highest form of human evolution all come together in its primary function to promote a deeper level of understanding among people. There is no other behavior that facilitates intimacy as quickly, no other form of communication that can so quickly express the essence of human experience.

In reviewing the various functions that crying serves in our lives, as biological as well as social and emotional beings, it is clear that regardless of its original purpose as a simple eye cleaner, it has become one of the most distinguishing features of what it means to be human. As we decipher the various meanings of tears in the chapters that follow, we must look beyond this behavior as a simple act disconnected from the emotions for which it speaks. There is a need to have our feelings acknowledged and responded to. This requires hearing not only the language of tears but also all the emotional parts of us that are crying out to be understood.

4

understanding
the meanings of tears

C rying was designed by Nature to serve us in a number of ways, related both to our physiological systems and to our interpersonal relationships. Yet, this behavior has meaning for us in a number of other ways—as a conscious awareness of our motives; as the unconscious, symbolic significance uncovered through dialogue with others; or as the unique expression of our individual perceptions of what is going on around us.

Although there are some universal meanings to tears in certain circumstances—such as grief reactions across all cultures—there is also a special way that each of us communicates in this medium. Sometimes we are talking to others in code, letting our tears say what we are unable to get across with words. Other times, we are speaking mainly to ourselves by a strange internal mechanism in which our bodies excrete water from our eyes to get our own attention. In all cases and circumstances, for each person tears have a special meaning that must be decoded in order to make sense of this arresting form of emotional expression.

One of the aspects of this subject that is so remarkable is the variety of things that can be said through crying, not only across cultures, geographical locations, and genders, but even by a single individual who is fluent in the language of tears. One such woman, a virtuoso in this mode of communication, illustrates some of the meanings that are evident in her weepy speech. This case also demonstrates the incredible benefits that can accrue by becoming more proficient in finding the significance in your own tears, as well as in those of others to whom you are closest.

I can still hear the sniffles and sobs of this woman who wouldn't talk much at all; she spoke only in the language of tears. Deep wails. Soundless body-wracking sobs. Helpless whimpers that seemed to have a life of their own.

I see her as vividly as if she was in the room with me this moment. This is no hallucination; it is merely the legacy of the power that tears can bring. I see them dripping from beneath the cascade of hair that is hiding her face, each one a statement of despair and helplessness. I know this because she looks the way I feel. I have tried everything that I can to reach out to her, to guide her through this ocean of tears. Yet she is drowning, going down for the third count, and pulling me under with her.

She has cried every time we have been together, sometimes for a complete hour, other times intermittently, like rain showers that fall in spurts. She cries in so many different ways that I have learned to recognize the vocabulary, the grammar and syntax, of her language. I can tell by the quantity and quality of her tearfulness whether she is feeling just a little sad, or downright suicidal. I can recognize the difference between listless tears that are sent out just to inform me she feels tired of what we are talking about, and passionate tears that make a dramatic statement about the depth of her feeling. I have seen, heard, and felt her shed tears of loss, grief, disappointment, despondency, frustration, anger, even relief and joy. She has taught me the special meanings that crying holds for her, even though she has been unable to put her feelings into words.

Even more important for her own sake, by understanding her own tears she was eventually able to come to terms with the toxic feelings that persisted in leaching out of her eyes. She was able to find some meaning in her crying, to decode the language her body was speaking. She understood how the tears had been trying to get her attention, to push her to make some changes in her life. To her own amazement, the faucet of despair stopped once she began to take some needed action. She no longer felt so powerless and helpless.

DIFFERENCES IN FLUENCY

This woman is unusual, both in the frequency, intensity, and extent to which she cried, and also in her motivation and ability to uncover the various meanings of her tears. Before you can hope to make sense of any behavior, you need a larger context in which to understand its significance. This includes not only the person's gender, culture, family, and background, but also some information about what is considered normative for that person. Each of us feels a different comfort level with our tears, a different willingness to cry under some circumstances but never in others. For the person who cries several times a week at the slightest provocation, this behavior has a different meaning than for someone who hardly ever sheds tears.

In their studies of this phenomenon, psychologists Jeanne Plas and Kathleen Hoover-Dempsey classified the characteristic reactions that people have to their own tears. They noted, for example, the difference between those who seem perfectly comfortable with their own tears and those of others, versus those who have no tolerance for this behavior whatsoever. Although these researchers were interested specifically in tears spilled in the workplace, the same themes are prevalent in any setting. Basically, most of us fall into one of several degrees of fluency.

The Empty Well

There are people who don't experience any emotions strong enough to precipitate tears. They are even-tempered and reveal relatively few signs of affect. Not only do they show little emotion on the outside, but when they are confronted by various experiences in life, their arousal levels on the inside remain very low. For example, when James Gross and two colleagues showed the film *Steel Magnolias* to a group of 150 women, they discovered that whereas 20 percent of the women cried spontaneously, there were others in the group who were moved very little by what they viewed, at least in terms of their somatic, respiratory, and cardiac activity.

Crying is irrelevant to this group because they never get emotionally aroused (or perhaps never allow themselves such arousal) to the point where crying responses are activated. Their hypothalamic and visceral activity idle at lower levels, even during periods of crisis. The muscular and endocrine systems that kick in during the excretion of tears never receive signals that they are needed; over time their functioning begins to atrophy.

Although this group is composed mostly of men, there are exceptions as well. One woman I interviewed is very much in touch with her inner feelings, but finds tears to be very rare in her life:

> I would *like* to cry the way others do. It's just that I never get to that point. I think I'm a fairly happy person and all, loving and affectionate toward my husband, children, and grandchildren, but I just don't ever get to the point where I cry. I have wondered if something is wrong with me, or whether I am missing something inside, but I have decided that this is just the way I am.

It is much more common that a feeling of emptiness is typical of those who are unable to access any emotional states inside themselves. It is as if there is some connection missing in their brain or limbic system, so that they are just not able to experience any strong feelings. This may be the result of some psychological trauma they suffered as children in which they now protect themselves by banishing all intensity from their lives. It may also be similar to a form of autism in children, or schizoid disorder in adults, in which there is an utter blankness, an emptiness inside.

Those in Denial

This group includes those who do have the capacity to cry . . . if they would allow it to happen. During those few occasions when tears inadvertently slip out, they do not acknowledge them: "I'm *not* upset! I just have something in my eye."

These individuals do experience intense feelings that they are able to ignore or deny on a cognitive level, usually beyond their awareness. As an example, a sixteen-year-old boy who had in his younger years been quite fluent in the expression of tears now belonged to a peer group in which such behavior was completely unacceptable. After being told by his girlfriend that she no longer wished to be with him, the young man could be seen doing everything within his powers to keep himself under control. At that moment, if you asked him what he was feeling, he would tell you with a shrug that he was not feeling much of anything: "Hey, it's no big deal. I was ready to end things myself." The giveaway, however, is the quivering lip and the moisture that is pooling under the lower lids of his eyes, evidence he quickly wipes away as he tries to go about his business.

Naturally, maintaining relationships with these types of individuals can be very difficult as they are unwilling or unable to articulate what they are feeling. They understand nothing about the language of tears. A dialogue with one such person sounded like this:

Therapist: What sparked those tears just now?
Client: [*Shrugs*]
Therapist: Well, I noticed something was going on with you that seemed pretty powerful.
Client: Yup.
Therapist: What might that have been?
Client: I don't really know.
Therapist: Don't know, or don't want to say?
Client: What's the difference?

Therapist: You tell me.

Client: [*Shrugs*]

Therapist: What do you suppose your tears were saying to me and to you?

Client: I suppose that I tend to compartmentalize things too much, that my family-of-origin issues are getting in the way.

Therapist: That's what your head is saying. What about your heart?

Client: [*Shrugs*]

Shame is a strong factor with these individuals. There is something within their self-definition, often related to their particular age, gender, and culture, that makes crying unacceptable. They might like to cry, but it is not an option they give themselves, except under the most extreme circumstances.

Submergence

We all know people like this, and can see them everywhere. These are the ones who have quivering lips, trembling cheeks, ragged breathing, even moist eyes, but they will not permit a tear to fall. Unlike those who are empty, these people do have strong feelings. And unlike those in denial, they are aware of these emotions even if they won't allow them to emerge.

In the first group, crying has no meaning because of the control over emotional activation that takes place on a physiological level. The second group learned through cultural conditioning to exert control through denial. This third group actually *chooses* on their own not to cry. They have all the equipment they need, in perfect working order, but are able to talk themselves into stifling the response.

Crying is often viewed by those in this group as messy. Why bother stirring things up? What is the use in making a spectacle of yourself? Depending on your orientation, they are either blessed or plagued by the ability to keep themselves under control. Indeed, it takes tremendous commitment and self-discipline to keep tear ducts under control. As one person admits: "I *could* cry, but I would rather not."

If you could get inside their heads during critical moments when they are feeling especially moved, you would hear something along the lines of the following: "Don't do it. Come on, get ahold of yourself! You'll look like an idiot. Your eyes will puff up. And it won't do any good anyway. Take a deep breath. Again. *Come on!* Don't let this get the best of you. The feeling will pass."

Private Moments

Even among those people who are regular criers, there are distinct preferences as to whether to cry privately or publicly. For some, crying is a profoundly personal experience, something that is only done when alone. For this type of crier, tears have little to do with communicating a message to anyone else. Rather, they are something you do for yourself, with yourself, by yourself. To these people, crying is kind of like any personal habit, such as touching your genitals, picking your nose, grooming yourself, or screaming in a soundproof room—a secret to be shared with nobody else.

For example, two people, side by side, are both crying at

a funeral. One feels a great sense of relief, even a sense of pride, that he is expressing himself clearly and honestly. He doesn't attempt to restrain his sobs. He doesn't even bother to wipe the tears away; they are symbols of how much he mourns his loss. The other person, however, feels terribly embarrassed by what he perceives as a loss of control on his part. He looks next to him at the guy who is blubbering incoherently, and then feels even more ashamed of himself. He does everything he can to hold himself back. Each tear that falls seems like a rebuke to his self-control. He feels miserable not only about his loss but also about his unseemly behavior that should have been restrained until he could be alone.

It is difficult to find private criers who are willing to talk about their experiences—for them, to do so is a violation of privacy as surely as talking about masturbation in public. "It is such a secret place, the land of tears," remarked Antoine de Saint Exupery in *The Little Prince.* Some people report that when they feel frustrated, angry, saddened, or overwhelmed, and it is neither convenient nor seemly to cry openly, they will hurry into a private place to shed tears. Just as we can almost always make it to a rest room during times of urgent need, so too can some people control their tear flow until it is safe. One woman describes this struggle:

> I much prefer to cry alone than in public. Some people have that no-biggie sort of cry where the tears just come out of their eyes, but they continue on just fine. With me, it's more like a whole body symphony or something where I can hardly speak and I look like hell. I just have to be alone when that happens. Otherwise, I'd scare the hell out of other people.

Indeed, there are many people who find a positive meaning in their tears only when they cry alone. Crying becomes for them a private conversation, one that loses its significance when in the presence of others. Likewise, there are quite a few other people walking around who cry when they are by themselves, not as an exercise in self-release or awareness but in utter despair similar to the woman whose story began this chapter. Unlike this woman, however, they hide the extent to which they are suffering, putting on a pleasant face for the benefit of the outside world. They feel desperately wounded inside, suffering mightily, but confide in no one about their pain. It becomes their deepest and darkest secret that once they are alone again, behind closed doors, the mask will fall as they dissolve into a pool of tears.

Acceptance

This is the group of freest criers who are totally fluent in their language of tears. They are readily able to express how they feel through all the various forms that were described in the previous chapters. Some of these individuals have reflected sufficiently on their tearfulness that they have been able to classify the forms in ways that might not immediately come to mind.

People who are in touch with their tears are more attuned to their innermost thoughts and feelings. According to Jeremy Safran and Leslie Greenberg, who have developed a whole system of therapy that works to help people process their emotional experiences, this awareness is central to good communication and solid relationships with others. After all, affective attunement (as it is called by some researchers) is the basis of empathy and intimacy between people. The extent to which you are sensitive to another person's feelings, and your own internal reactions to these feelings, is related to the quality of your mutual understanding.

Indeed, isn't it amazing when someone in your life can read instantly what you are feeling from the presence of a single tear, almost before you are quite aware yourself?

Whether between husband and wife, parent and child, therapist and client, or any two people who are attempting to communicate, empathic resonance results from being able to sense, read, feel, all the subtleties and contours of emotional experience. Perhaps most of all, tears are open to so many possible interpretations that deciphering their meaning becomes especially challenging.

MAKING SENSE OF TEARS

Difference in fluency is not the only variable that must be considered in finding the meaning in tears. In previous chapters, we have looked at the vocabulary of tears as if they represent discrete states of being that can be readily recognized, if not in yourself then at least in other people. To understand the meaning of this behavior, it makes sense that first you would have to identify accurately just which emotion is being spoken for. Obviously, tears convey quite different messages depending on whether they are representations of agony or ecstasy.

The problem with labeling the feeling that is being expressed and then decoding the language of the accompanying tears is that a number of other factors must also be considered, making things far more complex than would first appear.

Therefore, you will want to consider the following: how particular feelings that tears speak for become intermingled with reactions; how anything that you are crying for at one moment can so easily change to something quite different a moment later; how much of the time you don't really know exactly what you are feeling; and how the meaning of tears is derived from your perception of what is happening, a circumstance that is affected by unconscious distortions as well as deliberate judgments.

Mixed Emotions

Emotional reactions are often blended rather than discrete entities. Whereas the use of verbal language implies that feelings come in one of several distinct flavors, this does not accurately reflect reality. Someone asks how you are feeling, or why you are crying, and you often reply with a single response: sad, mad, or glad. Since this seems to satisfy the other person, rarely do you look beneath these simple labels to explore the complex combination of sensations, perceptions, thoughts, and feelings whirling around inside you.

A friend breaks off a relationship with you after a number of years. Look deep inside and you will note that you are feeling sad, relieved, ashamed, frustrated, misunderstood, angry, regretful, and confused, all at once. As you begin to reflect on what this ending relationship means for you, tears begin to fall down your cheeks. Which feeling are the tears speaking for?

An opportunity you were looking forward to falls through unexpectedly. You cry in disappointment over the lost chance, but also feel a total release of tension at the prospect of greater freedom now that you aren't locked into that commitment.

It is the norm that you feel ambivalent about almost everything that happens to you. It is typical that your tears speak for a half dozen different parts of you at the same time.

I Don't Know

For reasons that should already be evident, much of the time people don't really know what they are feeling. Considering the mixed and fickle nature of affective experience, it is no wonder.

We often make up simplistic answers to satisfy queries when we really have no idea what is going on inside us. Since it is a totally unacceptable answer to someone who asks why we are crying to say, "I don't know," instead we usually tell them (and ourselves) something that seems reasonable.

> I have an eighteen-year-old son who is in the process of moving out on his own. I'm glad that he's doing what he wants but I also have some concerns about him, and his move, which I brought to his attention. During this interaction, I cried most of the time. The tears were telling him how much I loved him. I want you to do well. I'm here for you when you need me.
>
> Yet the tears were also saying so much more—how much I will miss him. I'm afraid of the uncertainty that lies ahead for both of us. I was crying for him, but mostly for myself. I'm scared of what the future will bring.

It was at this point that this woman became lost, unable to articulate everything that she had been feeling at the time she was crying. It was not that she didn't know how she was feeling as much as she was aware of too much. Furthermore, this is not all that unusual. Much of the time it is difficult to state definitively what exactly you are feeling as tears are streaming down your face.

It is during such times that analytic reasoning processes tend not to be working at high levels. Crying is a time for feeling, not for thinking or making sense of what is going on.

What Is Real?

What you see isn't necessarily what is really happening. Previously, we looked at how crying can be used manipulatively to deceive others for personal gain. People work hard to disguise, or even hide, their true feelings. Why give someone the leverage of knowing your true intentions or reactions when by leading them astray you can win some advantage?

One contributing factor to the frequency with which we can't identify accurate emotional signals is that often what we are showing on our faces is not what we are really feeling. In one study conducted by psychologists Carol Barr and Robert Kleck, two-thirds of the people who were asked to rate their degree of expressiveness while watching funny film clips were surprised at how blank their faces actually looked on video of the session.

The distinction can thus be made between *real* crying and *pseudocrying*. The former tears are spontaneous, genuine, and heartfelt, whereas the other kind can be used manipulatively. One man I spoke with felt particular resentment toward this topic because he so mistrusts the validity of crying:

> With my two boys, who are four and seven, sometimes if they fall down or something, they will start crying because they think they are supposed to. They aren't really hurt or anything; they just want some attention. When they do that, or when my

wife cries, I am immediately mistrustful. If you want something from me, just ask for it; don't cry about it.

You can see quite clearly that the particular meaning that crying has for each person depends very much on the larger context of that person's previous experience on a number of fronts. People who are suspicious of others' tears, who don't trust them as genuine expressions of feeling, have either been burned in the past by deception or are quite skilled themselves at pseudocrying to get their way.

Good, Bad, and Ugly

The meaning of an event is related not only to what it is but also to the judgment as to whether it is a good or bad thing. This complicates matters further since deciding whether tears are helpful or harmful in a particular moment determines whether they should be encouraged or stopped.

People routinely classify their own tears in this way. As you sort through the variety of your own experiences, you will find that you have developed your own system to label the different ways that you cry. You may have a category of *good tears* and *bad tears,* the former resulting in a release of tension, the latter leading to feeling worse. Another grouping might include sentimental tears versus those that involve deep crying. In the first case, you are shedding a few tears in remembrance of the past, whereas in the second instance you are emotionally wrecked by an overwhelming experience in the present. You may also make distinctions between tears of pain and joy, depression and sadness, anger and frustration, between ceremonial crying and spontaneous reactions. Among all these different categories, the one that we use most readily is whether the tears are helpful or harmful.

UNDERSTANDING THE SIGNIFICANCE OF CRYING

The picture that is emerging is one in which crying can be seen to have different meanings depending on the frequency and fluency with which the person cries; the stability and purity of the feeling that the tears speak for; the clarity of a person's perception, influenced by both unconscious and intentional motives; the self-judgments about whether the experience is good or bad; and the symbolic significance within a given situation and culture.

We have also seen how tears represent both a form of language and a kind of physiological response to changing internal conditions. What this means is that in order to cry, three conditions must be met. First, you have to *be* sad or elated or dejected, meaning that this is a familiar experience to you, one you can recognize. Second, you have to perceive that state as existing in the present. Third, you have to be willing to show through your tears what you are experiencing privately.

In this section, we explore more deeply the significance of crying as a personal and social act. Before we sketch out some generalizations about what crying means for most people, we must first consider the source of the many misunderstandings that take place as a result of such individual differences.

Meanings and Misinterpretations

An act of crying, or any event for that matter, can have a different meaning for every individual who is part of, or who is observing, the experience. Thus, when we speak of the meaning of tears, we have to consider the perspectives of both the person who is communicating and the one who is interpreting the behavior. Often these two different meanings don't coincide, as in the case of a husband and wife who are in strong disagreement.

Most conflicts between people result from an inability or unwillingness to hear what the other person is saying. Nowhere is this more evident than in tearful communications, which we have learned are even more ambiguous and variable in their meaning than any other form of emotional expression. In this dialogue, two people are desperately trying to make contact with one another without much success:

Husband: So, I think that we should just let it go, I mean, I don't see how we could possibly . . .

Wife: [*Tears well up in the corner of her eyes. She averts her eyes, casually wiping her sleeve across them.*]

Husband: What? [*Silence*] What's wrong? [*More silence*] Look, if you think I should do something different, then just tell me.

Wife: [*She reaches for the tissue box, holds it on her lap. Her husband braces himself, as if he is about to get blown away.*] It is just . . . [*Tears flow in earnest now.*] just that . . . [*Sobs once, twice, then lets herself go.*]

Husband: Jesus! What did I do now? [*She sobs louder.*] Look, I'm sorry. Whatever I said or did, I didn't mean to. Come on. Give me a break! [*He is becoming angry.*]

Wife: It . . . it's not . . . that. I am trying [*Deep breath. Then another.*] I'm trying . . . I just can't . . . [*Breaks down in tears again.*]

Husband: If you can't talk about this, then I don't know
how we can expect to work this out.

Of course, she *is* talking, but her husband is not able to
hear what she is saying, nor find the meaning in her chosen
form of self-expression. After all, in his vocabulary of tears,
there are only two entries: "I am in excruciating agony and
will probably die," and "The Lions just won the Super Bowl!"
Yet, this woman has a varied range of things that she can communicate with her tears. Even though they have lived together
for eight years, they still haven't clarified what is meant by this
special form of communication.

In this brief interaction, for example, the husband at first
feels guilty because he interprets the tears as accusatory, that
he has done something wrong, something to hurt her. When
he recognizes that this is probably not what has happened,
then he becomes angry: "Why is she doing this? Why can't she
be more like me and say what she really means?" He is indignant because she is speaking a foreign language that he cannot understand.

It is difficult to understand or agree on the significance
of crying when two people have such different perceptions of
what is being communicated. Here are several other examples
of how two competing constructions of meaning are based on
different views of the person who is crying versus the person
who is listening:

What the Crier Says	*What the Listener Hears*
"I'm frustrated because you aren't understanding me."	"You are angry because you aren't getting your way."
"I want to be closer to you."	"You want to push me away."

"I'm hurting."   "You are trying to manipu-
                                   late me."

"I am so moved by your   "I have embarrassed you."
offer."

Like any form of communication, the language of tears
has greater potential to be misinterpreted when both parties
are not together in the ways they talk and listen to one another. Unless both people take the time to clarify what each
is saying and hearing, further misunderstandings will most
likely occur. Any consensus on meaning will remain elusive.

This situation is compounded by the reality that all
communications, whether verbal or nonverbal, take place on
multiple levels at the same time. In the examples of misunderstanding just mentioned, it is not so much that both the
crier and listener are saying or hearing one thing only; mixed
and often contradictory messages are being exchanged on
multiple levels.

Meaning on Different Levels

Finding meaning in what crying communicates involves decoding what is being expressed, both explicitly and implicitly.
This also involves understanding the context of the tearful
communication, as far as what preceded it.

Several decades ago, an interdisciplinary research team
led by Gregory Bateson looked at the interactions that take
place between people, especially those in dysfunctional families. They discovered a pattern that most of us are already well
aware of—all communications include both surface messages
(what is reported) and underlying messages (nonverbal cues).

Crying has meaning in the context of both levels in which it is expressed. On a surface level, tears convey nonverbal messages to alert either yourself or others that some emotional activation is taking place. The husband in the preceding example heard this message loud and clear: "My wife is troubled. She is feeling something very intensely." At the deeper level, however, there were other things being communicated that he was unable to follow. Depending on facial expression, body posture, spatial placement, vocal tone, and other cues, tears signal a number of possible messages from "Help me" to "Leave me alone"—and nearly everything in between.

Whereas confusion and frustration result when two people are not speaking the same language of tears, or when the crier can not make sense of what her own tears mean, quite wonderful things can happen when the particular meaning of the communication is sorted out. One man describes how, by attending to his own tears on different levels, he precipitated a breakthrough in his life. Prior to this particular turning point, he had been attending to his feelings purely on a surface level, never connecting them to events in the past, to unconscious reactions, to the underlying significance of being unable to cry:

> I learned to cry in a men's group I was attending to work on some pain I couldn't get through on my own. My father had sexually abused me when I was a boy and I had never really dealt with that stuff.

> Here I was an English teacher, a language artist, and yet I was mute; I couldn't express myself. Yet I marveled at how these other men—truck drivers, store clerks, and salesmen—could

give utterance to their innermost feelings. They spoke with such richness about their pain. And they cried.

I would choke with feeling for them but I couldn't do so for myself. Then one night when another guy was talking about his own abuse issues, I just lost it. I flooded over with tears remembering what had happened to me in the fifth and sixth grade. I had been so embarrassed by this I couldn't talk about it, but my tears spoke for me. They gave me the language to deal with the shame. Then I could put it behind me.

As this man so eloquently puts it, his tears grabbed him so that he could no longer ignore what was festering inside him. They forced him to look at issues he had been avoiding for a long time. They were the most tangible evidence, perhaps the only physical proof, that he was feeling something intensely inside. Prior to the incident in the group, meaning had been restricted for him to a superficial level where he had been unable to access the deeper significance of his feelings.

Symbolic Meanings of Crying

We are concerned not just with the overt meanings of things but also with their symbolic, unconscious, and disguised representations. Since tears have been mentioned so prominently in religious literature, mythology, popular songs, and other cultural artifacts, the analyst can have a field day generating possible interpretations.

Most obviously, tears are a bodily fluid excreted just like urine, saliva, sweat, or digestive juices. As such, crying may symbolically be viewed as part of the immune system, an aggressive defense against emotional trauma. Other symbolic interpretations are offered by psychoanalysts who see crying as a compensatory defense against other internal drives. In other words, the release of tears may be substituted for the discharge of sexual energy. For those who are too restricted and inhibited in their expression of passion through their genitals, releasing fluid through the eyes is seen as an alternative.

Other explanations have been offered that focus on tears as a depletion of body fluid. Both the crying infant and the depressed adult wait passively and helplessly for caregivers to replenish lost nourishment. It is as if the human body is a barrel filled to the brim with sloshing salt water. When a leak sends a stream of tears arching to the ground, it is a signal that someone must patch the hole and fill the barrel back to the top.

At its most basic symbolic level, crying is often an act of regression in which we retreat to the earliest preverbal stage of life. During a time before words, tears were the only way we could communicate distress. When we are experiencing grief or discomfort or arousal we become again our most basic selves.

Psychoanalysts Edwin and Constance Wood conceptualize crying, in all its permutations, as an expression of loss. It is a temporary loss of equilibrium between various instinctual drives. Consistent with this model of present behavior as being connected to unresolved issues in the past, psychoanalysts view tears as emotional regression triggered by something that evoked previous experience—such as a funeral, wedding, or movie scene. Whether consciously or beyond awareness, while our brains and psyches are busily recalling painful episodes (from birth trauma to yesterday's disappointment), tears communicate when verbal systems are overloaded. It is as if the television screen temporarily loses its visual image so the studio sends out a more basic signal.

As for the meaning of happy tears, they may be explained as the delay of affect. In one study, Joseph Weiss cites classic examples of this when someone cries at his own testimonial dinner, or a new immigrant weeps upon seeing the Statue of Liberty. The tears represent a release of feeling that has been held in check for years.

When feelings are too threatening for us to deal with at the time, if we have the choice we shelve them long enough for us to fortify ourselves. Whether you are living vicariously through a movie or novel or experiencing a loss directly, it is more often at the point of reunion and reconciliation that tears are finally released. Following Freud's theory of psychic energy, crying may symbolically represent the discharge of affect once it is safe to experience its full brunt.

A man has toiled for years in relative obscurity. He feels saddened by this lack of recognition, unappreciated and lonely. Yet he stuffs these feelings down and continues on with his work, doing the very best he can. He wants to cry, not only in frustration and hurt but also in anger. Instead, he redoubles his efforts, channels his psychic energy into greater drive to achieve. When he weeps openly at his retirement celebration, he is releasing thirty-five years of pent-up emotions.

Among all of these different theories that offer possible symbolic explanations to account for what tears mean, it is clear that this behavior is far more than external displays of internal processes. When you are crying, you are saying something *to* someone, even if it is to yourself.

Social Contexts for Constructing Meaning in Tears

Meaning is derived primarily within the context of interactions with others. Even among infants who are just a few weeks old, parents are well aware of what has been confirmed in research laboratories—that babies cry less when being held and more when physically apart from their mothers. Clearly the expression of tears is a social event, for the mother as well as the infant. In fact, one study found a mother's very image as a competent parent is directly related to her perceived ability to stop tears through her interventions. As it turns out, this concern may not be exaggerated. In a study conducted by Barry Lester, mothers who were more sensitive and skilled at reading their baby's cries have children who are better adjusted and more socially successful as they mature.

Research suggests that not just with infants but with any person who is in tears the meaning of this event can only be determined by considering the way others react. As in any form of communication, thousands of adjustments are made each second as we take in and process information about what is happening within us and around us. Depending on what people do before, during, and after tearful episodes, we may cry more or less intensely, longer or shorter, freely or with inhibition. This also means that if you want to decode what others' tears are saying to you, you will also have to examine your own behavior.

One man who is far more comfortable in the world of data and numbers than in the more subtle nuances of tears describes how he came to terms with what he once saw as his wife's overemotional nature:

I used to blame my wife for crying, as if it was her fault she was feeling so much. I wanted her to be more logical and rational in the way we had discussions. . . . Yes, I wanted her to be more like me.

It didn't come easy but I eventually realized that I was often the one who was making her cry even harder by withdrawing the way I did. Here she is reacting strongly to something, maybe one of our kids in trouble. She's crying. I'm hurting, too. I *can't* cry, so I start yelling at her to shut up so I can think. She cries harder. I then get even more angry, and I was never really upset with her to begin with, but my son won't listen to me, so I take it out on her instead.

Now that I try hard to listen to my wife instead of shutting her down, her crying helps both of us to talk about what is most disturbing.

Rarely can someone articulate so clearly the dynamics of circular interaction as they affect tearfulness in the context of a relationship. It is not uncommon in a relationship that one person (usually the woman or the one who is more emotionally expressive) will be *designated* to cry. In such cases, tears can be viewed not as the expression of a single person but *on behalf* of oneself and another, as in the case of the couple just described.

It is becoming increasingly apparent that tears are unparalleled as a powerful language system, a way to communicate the essence of a feeling, sometimes overriding all semblance of control. Tears heighten our awareness of self and others. They override cognition and rational decision making. They can dominate perception and interpretation of reality so completely that we could easily conclude that feelings *are* the essence of human experience.

Our ability to feel sadness, shame, anger, pity, compassion, or elation—vicariously or as direct experience—is the foundation of the empathy that connects us to others. To the extent that family and friends shared our tears during times of crisis, we were able to speak a common language, even if the dialects were sometimes indecipherable. Tears are part of the glue that bind us together.

In the first half of this book, we have looked at the meaning of crying, its many varieties and functions. We have developed a set of general principles to understand the language of tears. Yet just as a tongue such as Mandarin, English, Spanish, or French may be written roughly the same across a wide expanse of territory, there are many dialects of these languages. Each of them reflects a slightly altered set of rules regarding grammar, pronunciation, and contextual usage. This same linguistic difference can also be found in the communication of tears—each culture has a distinctly different accent in its tears.

5

crying across cultures

T he language of tears is hardly a universal form of communication in every part of the world. People from different places speak unique dialects in their tearfulness
and have different attitudes toward emotional expression. Each
society operates from a particular set of values, religious beliefs,
family traditions, and interactive rules, which are applied to
communication of all sorts. If, for example, we were to attend
a funeral in New Guinea, Ghana, Taiwan, Quebec, Peru, or Ire-
land, would we recognize a familiar pattern of weeping? Surely
we would notice some differences in this behavior, but would
these variations be significant or simply minor adaptations?

In this chapter, we will be visiting a number of different
regions, examining their views on crying but mostly looking
at the distinct ways they speak through their tears. Some of
these patterns will be familiar to you, while others may seem
quite strange. As a preview, for example, consider the crying
of the Makonde, a Bantu people of Tanzania. They speak a different language of tears, one that is higher in tone than we are
used to. Rather than the continuous tears that we send out,
they cry in short, loud, high-pitched, explosive bursts, almost
like a siren.

A missionary couple I spoke with described the difficulties they encountered learning to cry at funerals of their new Tanzanian friends so they would not stand out. The woman cried into a tissue, which the Makonde found strange. They wondered why not just let the tears fall? They were even more puzzled by the man crying into a handkerchief he then replaced in his pocket. They wished to know why he was saving the expulsions from his eyes and nose. Did they have some special meaning?

One of the most fascinating aspects of research into this subject has been to examine the ways that crying is treated in places that are far removed geographically and philosophically from our own vantage point. A given culture's language of tears says a lot about the emphasis it places on self-restraint versus self-expression and emotional intimacy. In some ways, the language of tears is an extension of a culture's native tongue.

CRYING AS A CULTURAL EVENT

Anyone who has spent much time living in another culture will recall the kinds of internal changes that result from this kind of immersion. Observing Italians passionately ogling a female pedestrian, or English reticence embodied in the wooden-postured guards in front of Buckingham Palace, or an African village erupting in grief over the loss of a loved one, can have a profound effect on your own propensity to display or restrict emotions.

Indeed, there is some basis for these impressions we have that the peoples of various cultures not only speak differently but also express themselves in a unique language of tears. One man who had just returned from a six-month stay in South America remarked on his own internal changes:

> I began to notice, first of all, how much more emotional I felt, and expressive I became, when communicating in the Spanish language. In part, this resulted from trying to fill in an inadequate verbal vocabulary with nonverbal emotional language, but my personality was definitely more passionate. My own tears felt closer to the surface than I am ordinarily accustomed.
>
> Once I returned home to the States, I forgot all about the personality transformation I experienced in my Spanish versus English self. It wasn't until I was talking to my friend who had also just returned from Latin America that I noticed the difference.

A woman then joined in the discussion by talking about how difficult it was for her to restrain herself emotionally in the United States:

> As a child I grew up in South America, where tears were a natural and honest response to something that happened. When I arrived in this country I learned very quickly that tears have quite a different meaning that puts you in a one-down position.
>
> It was like playing a game of chicken: as soon as I cried, I lost. I felt humiliated. Crying became associated with the negative aspects of my femininity.
>
> In this culture, showing emotions is viewed as a sign of weakness, but where I come from "machismo" is associated with passionate, volatile, explosive feelings.

In our discussions thus far, we have been considering crying as a natural phenomenon, one that is automatically elicited by universal triggers that occur on a daily basis. These can be biological events, like chemical imbalances in the body or toxic fumes in the environment. They can also be psychological events that include humiliation, rejection, anger, joy, or fear. Both in this chapter on cultural differences in crying and in the next two chapters on gender, we are expanding our orientation to consider this behavior as it has been socially conditioned. Emotions may often be not so much biological events as cultural performances, that is, learned responses to particular situations.

Norms and expectations in every society shape the way its citizens react to events. Some cultures encourage tearful expression as healthy and socially appropriate in certain circumstances, while others suppress crying with a vengeance. Therefore, each people has a belief about various kinds of emotional expression. How do we account for the differences among cultures of central Malaysia in which one tribe, the Chewong, have a total of eight references in their vocabulary to any state of feeling, whereas other peoples just down the road have more than two hundred words to describe states of emotion? How else do we explain that within a few miles of one another, three different Indonesian cultures display such different types of crying in response to grief?

Cultural Scripts and Rites of Tearful Passage

The very first place to look for evidence of established patterns in crying behavior is in a culture's prescribed norms and rituals. In all regions, various institutions of religion, education, government, or entertainment play a role indoctrinating citizens into appropriate scripts to play out in certain circumstances. While not all societies have access to television as a guide, they do have other forms of storytelling (music, dance, plays, myths, murals) in which model characters are observed facing struggles and then responding in sanctioned ways.

A collection of villagers in the Amazon basin of Brazil sit around a fire telling stories about the youngest tribesmen who just returned from a hunt in which not all who ventured out returned unscathed. One of the hunters was killed and a few others permanently crippled during a clash with another tribe over the limited supply of game. During the telling of story, the narrators are careful to portray the martyred ones as fearless warriors who shed not a tear for themselves or their loved ones.

The children listen enraptured by these tales of bravery, amazed at the self-control that was necessary for their relatives and neighbors to travel such great distances while wounded and all the while refusing to make a sound of protest. Of course, what really happened during this journey is beside the point—the children are learning the lesson that courage is equated with emotional restraint. It is one thing for a warrior to be wounded in battle, quite another feat for him to suffer without crying in pain.

Halfway around the world, the same process of cultural indoctrination takes place through a different medium. In an episode of a weekly television drama, we observe a little boy who is crying hysterically after being left at school. Then he is told that big boys don't cry. He gathers himself together, takes a deep breath, joins his mates, and is rewarded for his efforts by being viewed as instantly popular. The lesson of this cultural script is hardly lost on the youngest of viewers, who nods to himself with resolve that under similar circumstances he would act with similar dignity.

However much our emotions and tears may feel under our own control, we are actually permitted to cry only according to normative rules. How you react to someone who verbally attacks you depends on the setting. If it was the culture of your home, you might very well scream back or break down in tears. But if you were at work, you would most likely employ a more moderate response. Other cultural scripts dictate a different set of options. When faced with threat, a member of an Eskimo tribe would shrug and walk away from the disturbance, while people of other cultures might strike out violently or break into tears.

In a cross-cultural study examining how East African tribes respond to tears as compared to our own patterns, Sara Harkness and Charles Super noted that learning how and when to cry is similar to language acquisition in general. In other words, emotions are socialized by teaching grammatical rules that are enforced and corrected as deviations from expected norms take place.

One dramatic example of this is found in the circumcision ceremonies for both boys and girls that are not only considered as initiation rites into adulthood in parts of Africa, but major focal points of village solidarity. In preparation for these rituals, feasts are known to last for days. During the excruciating pain that accompanies genital mutilation during a time in life when senses are heightened, both boys and girls are expected to endure this procedure with dignity. Crying, in particular, is absolutely forbidden, bringing disgrace not only to the individual but to his or her family and community. Any chance of a good marriage or attaining a high position in the community would be ruled out if the victim should shed tears.

It is interesting how young people in the Western highlands of Kenya are scripted into muting their tears, even during times when the most courageous would cry. Harkness and Super contrast two different examples of how the language of tears is acquired through mother-child interactions. In the first case, Douglas, a Kenyan boy of thirteen months, is building a tower gleefully. When the blocks unexpectedly fall down, he bursts into tears. His mother interrupts immediately by saying: "Don't feel bad. I know you're angry. It's frustrating to build such a tall tower. There, there, try again." The mother quickly helps the child to identify what he is feeling, thereby guiding him to communicate in ways other than through tears. Next, she explains what caused this emotion and tells him that it is normal to feel this way. Lastly, she redirects her son to face the activity once again. Crying is interpreted as a signal that a challenge must be faced.

By contrast, in the second example, Kipkirui, age seven, wants to share the water his older sister is using to wash her hands. She refuses. They struggle until he ends up on the ground in tears. Kipkirui's mother scolds the sister, then admonishes the boy to keep quiet. She then recruits him to help prepare lunch.

While the ages and circumstances of these two boys are different, what transpired is consistent with how tears are responded to in the Kenyan Highlands. Among these people, crying is avoided or distracted from rather than attended to.

This is the mechanism that teaches emotional blocking, which will prove to be a crucial skill come the time when the knife starts cutting.

With respect to crying in response to pain, physicians have noted that members of particular ethnic groups react in consistent ways, based on the cultural scripts they are following. Italians and Jews, for example, are far more likely to be emotionally expressive than other groups. The English, Swedish, and Germans are going to cry considerably less often and intensely than those who originate from Mediterranean countries. This often results from how internal strength of character is defined by these cultures. To an Italian or Jew, there is no major loss of face associated with crying; in fact, there is an honorable tradition to weep openly during times of anguish. One Jewish proverb describes tears as the soap that washes the soul. During the Passover Seder, in which Jews celebrate the escape from Egyptian slavery, one ritual involves symbolically honoring the tears of bondage that were shed by bringing salt water to the lips.

The British, in contrast, are renowned for their emotional restraint, representative of their pride in keeping feelings to themselves. English philosopher John Locke wrote a treatise on the subject of tears, equating it with the ultimate in uncivilized behavior: "Crying is a fault that should not be tolerated in children; not only for the unpleasant and unbecoming noise it fills the house with, but for more considerable reasons, in reference to the children themselves; which is to be our aim in education."

Locke identified two kinds of crying, both pretty despicable: stubborn and domineering or querulous and whining. It was his contention that the first variety, based in obstinacy, should never be tolerated, as passion and desire must be subdued. The complaining kind Locke equated with "effeminacy of the spirit," which must be prevented or cured at all costs.

Yet, the culture that sparked Locke's pronouncements regarding the necessary restraint of tears has loosened just a bit over time. Only one generation after Locke's era, journalist Leigh Hunt acknowledged: "There are griefs so gentle in their very nature that it would be worse than false heroism to refuse them a tear." I suppose one tear is better than none at all.

When Cultures Cry

There are differences not only in the frequency with which people of various regions are inclined to cry but also in the specific situations in which tears may arise. An interdisciplinary and multicultural team of scholars from Switzerland, Japan, Germany, Israel, the United States, England, and France united in their efforts to compare how emotions are experienced differently in their respective countries.

Tears of sadness, for example, were more likely to result from relationship problems in Japan, whereas in Western cultures death or separation from a loved one produced the most profound distress. This is explained, in part, because separation due to divorce and relocation are more common in North America than in Japan, where people tend to remain throughout their lives in the vicinity where they were born. The researchers also noted that 20 percent of all sad experiences reported in the United States are due to the death of a loved one; only 5 percent are reported in Japan. This may be due to the different views of death encouraged by Eastern and Western religions.

In almost all cultures, the death of a child elicits crying. There are always exceptions, however, depending on how the people interpret the sequence of events. If, for instance, the death is blamed on witchcraft, anger might arise instead of tearfulness. If it is believed the little soul is on its way to a better place in heaven, then perhaps even happiness might result.

You would not have to travel halfway across the world to note such differences. Among Asian Americans you would observe much internal restraint in the expression of grief, whereas African-Americans and Native Americans have been enculturated to express feelings of loss through the fluent expression of tears. Each of these North American subcultures literally trains its members in the specific rules as to when and under what circumstances it is appropriate to cry. For example, once a Hispanic male reaches early adolescence, the concept of machismo makes it very difficult to express emotions thereafter through tears; anger is the sanctioned response to disappointment or loss.

In each of these cases, and any others that could be discussed, crying exists in a cultural context that is affected by the way events are defined (good, bad, or indifferent), and by rules for the way feelings should be expressed (stoic restraint, howls, wails, or silent tears). Anger, for example, might in some cultures be displayed through a sinister smile, while in others a war cry or sneer might be the usual form of display.

When Karl Heider studied the emotional reactions of cultures in Indonesia, he confirmed this idea that tears and other emotions are expressed in the context of language. He cites one example of how the vocabulary of feelings available to the Javanese Minangkabu of Sumatra and the Minangkabu of Indonesia dictate how members of each society experience sadness. He noted the distinctly different ways they reported coping with grief and sadness.

Concentrating on the culture of the Indonesian Minangkabu, one citizen describes how his people are absolutely forbidden to weep or show any signs of emotional sadness; they have but two choices—either to sing of their difficulties or to take their troubles on a private journey. It is interesting to note, however, that the reality of the situation is quite different from the cultural rules disclosed to strangers. In fact, people in all the Indonesian cultures react tearfully to sadness just as we would in our culture.

One conclusion drawn from this study is that although there are wide differences in how humans in different cultures interpret events and display their reactions, there are a few relatively universal emotional reactions, crying among them. Another thing to keep in mind as a student of tears is that what people say they do may be quite different from how they actually behave.

For example, one Pacific Islander described his people as passionate criers during times of grief and loss. He was highly critical of how emotionally restrained people of European ancestry were, using polite phrases such as "I'm so sorry for your loss" to substitute for more genuine feelings expressed through tears.

When actually witnessing the grief ceremony that accompanied the loss of a loved one, however, although there was indeed a room full of people crying, they were doing so in two very different modes. The first group of immediate family and close friends to the deceased would not appear all that unusual to our eyes and ears. The extent of wails, sobs, and flow of tears might be considered excessive by the standards of upper middle class Protestants, but would not be out of the ordinary for many other cultural groups that are known for being emotionally fluent. What would appear to be unusual, however, is a second group of acquaintances who are also crying, but in a tone and manner that suggests this is a contrived rather than genuine display of actual loss—these tears are the equivalent of polite words.

Grief Reactions

Grief presents us with one situation in which we can more easily make comparisons between cultural responses. In every part of the world, people die—and when they do, there is some process of saying goodbye to the departed. In a study of grief and mourning in seventy-eight cultures, Paul Rosenblatt and his colleagues sought to make some generalizations about how humans react to death. There are certain universal observations, for example, that humans build strong attachments to one another over time, and that the loss of these connections is quite distressing.

Bereavement thus leads to a number of powerful emotional reactions, among them sadness, loneliness, guilt, anger, fear, anxiety, and shame. All cultures have death customs that are provided on behalf of the deceased, to ease the passage from the living to the dead, and mostly for the benefit of those who are left to grieve. The primary intent of these rituals is to help people to work through their feelings in such a way that they may return to productive activities that serve the community.

Among the peoples of the world, the single most universal behavior that is expressed during grief is crying. Only the Balinese do not often shed tears, a curious phenomenon that was found to be related to their unique Hindu religious practices of remaining tranquil and unperturbed when in the face of tragic loss. When Rosenblatt visited Bali for a month to study the absence of tears further, he discovered that occasionally children would appear to make crying noises, but with the absence of tears. During one representative interview with a man who had lost three of his children, he smiled and laughed throughout the story, as if to say: "This is how I stop myself from crying."

Dramatic and uninhibited crying and wailing is more the norm for expressing grief around the world than our own disciplined tears. This is certainly the case with respect to the grief ceremony of the Maori people of New Zealand. The *tangi* is a kind of funeral ceremony in which all members of the family and community gather together to honor the departed. It is an intensely emotional experience in which participants use tears to demonstrate their grief and show the family how much they care. As was mentioned in the previous example of the Pacific Islander, it is expected that if you are truly sorry for the bereaved ones' loss, then show it with your eyes, not your mouth.

Ceremonies of Tears

It is instructive to compare how other cultures, different from our own, use tears as part of various rituals. Our own mourning customs have been designed specifically to inhibit tendencies toward aggression in the aftermath of a loved one's death. We can't have people acting out their grief and anger violently every time they experience a loss. Chaos would result. From the moment of the deceased's last breath, every subsequent movement of the bereaved is choreographed along predictable paths. Doctors, nurses, ministers, priests, rabbis, older family members, especially funeral directors, tell us exactly how to behave. Our lives are taken over by prescribed rituals.

Aggression is suppressed or sublimated quite differently in other cultures. Anthropologist Edward Schieffelin lived among the Bosavi people of New Guinea to study their ceremonies. One such ritual that has particular relevance to the subject of tears involves the systematic stimulation of weeping. Whenever guests from afar visit a village, they are expected to perform a night of dancing and singing for their hosts. All of a sudden, one among the villagers will grab a torch and proceed to burn the shoulders of the dancers, who will neither protest nor show pain. Among the villagers, however, anguish will be rampant—howling and weeping all through the night. The guests will then pay compensation to the villagers for causing them to cry. Success of the ritual is judged primarily on the basis of how long and how well people cried.

This is a ceremony of grief, of violence, of tribute and reciprocity. Mostly, it is about nostalgic tragedies. The object of this exercise is to elicit strong emotional reactions in the participants, to make them cry. The people themselves do not see any overt hostility, violence, or anger in their behavior. In the words of one researcher: "They see them as grand and exciting, deeply affecting, beautiful and sad, but not antagonistic. The songs are presented, not as taunts or mockery of the listeners, but in the same spirit of sympathy with which the guests themselves weep at the end of the ceremony for their friends and relatives among the hosts who have suffered."

It is the same in our culture. Are we not inclined to attend tragic films, plays, operas, and shows that make us weep? And are we not shedding tears as much for ourselves and our loved ones as for imaginary characters we have only just met?

Both within the culture of the Bosavi and in our own community, we have institutionalized "tear ceremonies" that help us to reflect on our feelings about our own existence through the lives of others. Songs and dances tell stories of lost love, making us cry. However barbaric we might find burning the shoulders of guests who have come to visit, isn't that what the representative gladiators of our cities attempt to do to the visiting football teams of our neighbors? So many of our spectator sports—boxing, hockey, rugby, and football—allow observers to live out their violent fantasies without getting hurt. It is the same with tears in many cultures—ceremonies and rituals are created that permit citizens to experience their emotions safely, without upsetting things too much. Nowhere is this more evident than during times of death.

A Case of Tuneful Weeping

Cultural differences in crying are not only evident in ceremonies of tears or death. In northern India, there are several communities in which weeping is regularly employed as a form of communication. First of all, there are distinctly different speech patterns between the men and women in the villages of this region. They use different tone and pitch variations, even different gestures.

When it comes to expressing emotion, the women have one set of swear words, exclamations, and verbal insults, while the men have another. The boundary between this gender-driven mode of expression is so rigidly defined that social ostracism would take place if, for example, a man used a speech pattern characteristic of women.

One of the communication options available only to women in this culture is that of *tuneful weeping,* not to be confused with the emotional crying that is common to both sexes among these people. This type of weeping, as a language system, contains actual wept statements, messages that are neither spoken nor gestured but conveyed through the rich emotional sights and sounds of tearfulness. It is a kind of poetic or musical language with its own syntax, grammar, and vocabulary.

After a daughter's wedding, for example, the mother communicates through tuneful weeping her sorrow and joy at the prospect of the young woman moving to her new husband's village. In fact, this is the only form of communication that is employed.

As each of the women of the village bids farewell to the newlywed, the bride greets each woman by crying on her shoulder. They then envelop one another in a sitting embrace, alternately and in harmony weeping together for five to fifteen minutes, depending on their degree of intimacy. The elder woman is always the one to stop first, persuading the bride to do so as well. The bride will then resist this admonishment, continuing to weep and thereby demonstrating her affection and respect.

This crying is hardly chaotic and disorganized. Each wept statement has its own structure and message, complete with a refrain made up of the customary term of address for that person—aunt, grandmother, wife of a brother, sister of a friend. Typically, the young woman wails her apologies for not having been more dutiful, or she may weep in humility for past transgressions, begging forgiveness. She begs to be always remembered in the village and hears in return a chorus of reassurance that she will not be forgotten.

Meanwhile, the men are not permitted to weep tunefully, but they may cry silently, moved by this spectacle of love and loss. They communicate their own feelings by calmly and politely asking the woman to cease her tears (which she will ignore). They will also pledge their allegiance to her, a promise to keep her memory and spirit alive.

Women rely on this form of communication whenever reunions take place and good friends who have been separated once again reaffirm their love and loyalty. They also use it when they have been wronged, articulating grievances through their tears and wails.

Nguch and Angst

From the preceding examples, it can be seen that crying is not so much a separate language as one that is tied to customs of verbal speech. Depending on the names that are given to describe internal states of feeling, very different responses could result. Crying thus occurs when a particular culture labels an emotion in such a way that the felt experience is one of sadness or shame rather than fatigue or anger.

Imagine, for example, that in the middle of a passionate speech in which you are speaking from your heart, someone interrupts you by implying that you are uninformed, misguided, and plain stupid. In any culture of the world, there would likely be some physiological activation taking place within the speaker's body. The key factor here is what you would call the feeling that you are experiencing. An Asian would feel shame, bowing his head in humiliation. A Latino might describe the sensations as anger, thereby cuing an indignant response. Every culture teaches its members to associate particular words with corresponding feelings, thereby programming sanctioned responses.

Anthropologist Robert Levy demonstrates the way the norms of a particular culture regulate the expression of feeling through the case of how Tahitians label their experience. In Tahiti, just as in our culture, people do feel states of grief, sadness, depression, and loneliness—the emotional conditions that we usually associate with crying. However, they describe these experiences as resembling a kind of bodily fatigue or sickness rather than as psychological distress. Because Tahitians label their feelings in this way, they are not inclined to cry in response to the same things that we would.

We can learn much about a given culture by the number of words they use to describe specific feelings. This gives us an indication as to how important this emotion is to a particular people, and which situations are mostly likely to elicit tears. For instance, some cultures have no word for guilt or shame, meaning that its members would never cry tears of humiliation. Yet, in our world we have a host of options to describe what is commonly experienced as shameful, embarrassing, ridiculous, disgraceful, dishonorable; we can feel guilty, abashed, mortified, humiliated. . . . With so many words to describe this feeling, it is a good bet that crying is a common response.

Anthropologists have often been puzzled about why the peoples of some cultures don't cry in response to the same things that we do. The answer to this mystery seems to be found in the presence or absence of particular words that are included as part of thought and speech patterns. Having done field studies with South Pacific Ifaluk people, anthropologist Catherine Lutz has noted a unique vocabulary to describe feelings consistent with their values. The word *nguch,* roughly translated as tired or bored, is one such term that has no exact equivalent in English. She cites examples of its use: a woman who is *nguch* of all the people who ask for cigarettes; a woman who said she was *nguch* after working at food preparation all day—"If I were a child, I would cry"; two women who were heard singing love songs as they walked were described as doing that so their *nguch* would leave them.

After a detailed linguistic analysis of that word usage, Lutz concluded that to be able to understand and use that emotion word appropriately, one has to assume an Ifaluk approach to the world. In our culture, we do not cry from *nguch* because the concept is unknown to us—which does not mean we don't experience feelings of ennui, listlessness, or being sick and tired of something.

Another example is the German word *angst,* which has invaded our psychologically sophisticated vocabularies. Introduced to us by existential philosophers, angst also has no direct English equivalent. It is similar to dread, or a kind of free-floating anxiety that gets at the core of being human and facing our essential aloneness. No matter what illusions we entertain, or how hard we try to make contact with others, nobody can ever get inside our skin and know what we are experiencing.

This angst-driven separation is magnified by the realization of our own imminent demise. If not this instant, then one in the not-too-distant future, your heart will cease beating forever. Thinking about this, or worse, feeling your fragile solitary place on Earth, is unnerving if not terrifying. This is angst, the anxiety we live with as part of being human.

Even if you don't have a word for angst in your emotional vocabulary, the feelings still lurk beneath the surface. It is the language of emotion, however, that brings these feelings into awareness, that gives them meaning. The tears that result from this awareness, whether they emerge out of guilt, nguch, or angst, occur within a cultural context. We are not born with the tendency to cry at these particular times; careful training by parents and others cue us as to how to react in almost every circumstance.

CORPORATE AND PROFESSIONAL CULTURES

The definition of culture includes not only the norms that exist within a particular geographical, religious, or racial group but also those that exist within any setting in which patterns of crying are established. When, where, and how people cry depends not only on their ethnicity but also on their social class, economic conditions, and professional affiliation. It means very little to talk about the ways that Irish Americans, African-Americans, or Italian Americans tend to cry, unless we consider other significant variables.

In North America, a far better predictor of crying behavior is not your cultural or religious background but rather your social class, education, and occupation. The more educated you are, the more flexibly you define your gender role, the more you work in a people-oriented job, the more likely it is that you will cry in response to a greater variety of situations.

There are cultural norms for crying that originate in your religious beliefs. Corporations have their own unique cultures. Even your family has a culture or set of rules about what is socially appropriate and what is unacceptable.

There is a cultural context to various professions and work settings as well. Therapists cry. A lot. Engineers don't. Stockbrokers don't, although they often feel like it. Truck drivers don't cry (except in country-and-western songs). Soldiers don't generally cry unless they reach a place of prominence in which they are permitted to do so on behalf of all the others who would like to weep. Nurses cry. Nurses *have* to cry in order to deal with the pain they get so close to. Doctors, however, rarely cry. They insulate themselves from pain—their own as well as that of their patients.

Besides your occupational setting, there are other cultural forces working in concert to shape when and how you respond emotionally to any event in your life. For example, you just opened a letter telling you bad news, *awful* news actually. You feel devastated. You can feel yourself choke up, your eyes fill up with tears—all of this happened in a few seconds, without conscious intent. Now, do you let yourself cry or not? And if so, how freely will you let yourself go?

The answers to these questions depend on where you are and who you are with. There are cultural norms for restaurants that are different from those for the office, your parents' house, your spouse's arms, or your own bedroom. Additionally, you can hear voices and see images from the past that influence what you do. Your parents gave you clear messages as to when they believed it was appropriate for you to cry and when it was not. There are rules established by your circle of friends and co-workers, policies that have been established over time. Movies and television shows have also provided models for this conduct. Our whole lives we have been indoctrinated into templates that guide us in our choices for how to respond.

So, there you stand, ready to cry, wanting to cry, needing to cry, but first you look around to see where you are. You also have flashbacks to those you remember having seen in similar predicaments. In an instant your brain calculates the potential risks and gains of giving the go ahead. The tears wait patiently: "So, are we to sit here all day? Will you be needing us or not?"

Cultural norms for crying, whether established by society, a tribe, or a family, guide (to use a gentle word) us in our behavior. A particular culture dictates rules as to how emotions should be restrained or expressed. These norms are related not only to the particular mode of communication—that is, to whether sadness results in stoicism or tears—but more deeply, to which feelings are actually experienced.

What all this means is that in order to make crying more

socially acceptable it is necessary to continue redefining what it means to be strong and competent. The obsolete vision of strength in the mold of emotional restriction is coming to an end. There is evidence all around you of more flexible, androgenous gender roles, a blending of different cultures, that allow for men to be more tearful when they choose, and for women to select other, less-vulnerable roles.

One of the more compelling images from the aftermath of the supposed "trial of the century" was a press conference in which O. J. Simpson's prosecutors faced reporters. There stood Marcia Clark, the woman and mother, stoic and restrained, while her partner Chris Darden, an African-American male, choked on his tears. Even more amazing evidence of the changing rules for tears in our culture, Darden was viewed favorably by the public for showing his feelings so genuinely.

In spite of the tendencies on the part of various peoples to react tearfully in uniform ways, there is a tremendous variation in this behavior. It is a mistake to overgeneralize by assuming that because someone is a member of a particular culture she is inclined to cry in particular ways. In fact, the differences among members of the same culture are often greater than those between different cultures.

It is difficult, if not downright deceptive, to look at tearful behavior without considering the microcultures that exist within particular homes, regions, communities, and genders. More than any other single variable, whether you are male or female dictates how and when you are likely to cry.

6

women and tears

Women are far more fluent than men in the language of tears. They are much more emotionally expressive, far more likely to cry, and when they do, it is for longer periods of time.

Women's faces are more expressive than men's. They are better skilled at sending nonverbal messages that are read accurately, and they display more cues more often than men do. Women are also better able to detect other people's inner feelings from limited visual cues. These characteristics are not only related to nonverbal facial expressiveness; when voice and words are added to the picture, the superior communication skills of women are even more significant.

Male and female infants start out on even ground, capable of reading and expressing emotions about equally. But by nursery school, girls show a small advantage over boys in this dimension, and the difference builds over time. Interestingly, this may not be the result of girls getting better at emotional expression as they age but rather of boys getting worse. Through biological and enculturation processes that begin when they are infants, boys' capacities in this area begin to atrophy over time.

In this chapter and the one that follows, we will examine some of the differences between the ways men and women express themselves through tears, and the reasons that account for these distinct dialects. There are genetic, biochemical, hormonal, and neurological factors involved, yet just as important are the social and cultural influences that play a role.

DIFFERENCES IN GENDER

Some of the things that we know about gender differences that affect crying behavior are that

- Girls are predisposed to verbalize language earlier than boys; they also master the intricacies of nonverbal communication to a greater extent.
- Boys are more nonverbally and behaviorally expressive as infants, causing parents to exert more control to stifle this intensity and girls to amplify their feelings in order to be heard.
- Peer socialization shapes females to externalize feelings and males to internalize them—to "act like a man."
- Boys play in larger, more competitive groups than girls, and teasing, criticism, and status are more prevalent in boys' groups than cooperation and emotional expressiveness.
- Girls learn to express feelings with words, tears, and gestures; boys learn to express themselves through behavioral action.
- Men express feelings primarily related to autonomy and separation (pride, anger, honor), while women express

feelings related to social bonding (guilt, shame, sadness, pity, fear).

- Physiologically and biochemically, women are better equipped to cry, not only in the ways their tear ducts are constructed but in the chemical and hormonal "fuel" that makes crying possible.

Each of these points only confirms what you already know: the gender differences evident in crying behavior are significant and dramatic. Crying is more adaptive for women just as anger is more likely to work for men to get them what they want. Historically, each gender plays a different role in society and therefore needs different tools to get their needs met.

In discussing gender differences related to crying, however, we need to be aware of the impact that feminism has had recently in balancing the influence of male-dominated values in our culture. While much of this attention to male and female differences in communication styles has been constructive, it has become politically correct to glorify everything that is feminine and denigrate all that is masculine.

For example, in an article that appeared in *Psychology Today,* gender differences in humor were singled out, with predicable results. Men's humor was described as aggressive, hostile, sarcastic, victimizing, mistrustful, and negative, making some people feel good at the expense of others. Women's humor, on the other hand, was described as everything that is wonderful—cooperative, caring, powerful, and positive, bringing people together by making them feel good. Of course, there is some basis for this observation, especially when comparing the angry, sexist, racist style of many male jokes to those favored by women.

But there is a tendency to make too much of gender differences, as if—to paraphrase the title of one best seller—women really are from Venus, and men from Mars, separate races from separate planets. While feminist theory has helped to empower women in a world dominated by patriarchal values, it has also led to greater divisiveness and tension rather than mutual understanding. At a recent dinner, I overheard one woman tell another that all men are liars. When I suggested she might be exaggerating, that certainly women lie as often as men do, she accused me of being defensive. And these were friends of mine!

In speaking of the increased conflict and tension between genders arising from the emphasis on differences, as well as from the changes in power, Diana Trilling notes: "We live in a world which runs with the blood of hostility between racial and religious groups, between ethnic and national groups. To these lamentable separations among people, we now add another division, a separation of sexes."

With this warning in mind, I approach the subject of crying as a distinguishing characteristic of gender with a degree of caution. While there are certainly anatomical and behavioral differences between men and women, we do share our humanity. Although women are demonstrably superior in certain areas (fine motor coordination, verbal skills, emotional sensitivity) and men in others (physical strength and speed, quantitative skills), we are more alike than we are different.

Women may cry more often on the outside but we

all feel like crying about the same number of times. It is gender training that molds us to express ourselves in particular ways.

Unique Languages of Men and Women

Boys and girls operate from different rules when it comes to expressing emotions. Anger is one such example in which males express their fear outwardly, through fierceness and aggression, while females are inclined to turn their fear inward in the form of tears. Boys learn to hide their hurt while girls learn to express it. Each of these strategies is adaptive in different ways, given the traditional gender roles.

In studies of gender differences with regard to emotional expression, the obvious is confirmed: women are expected to restrain their anger; to do otherwise is to be labeled hysterical or overemotional. John Nicholson describes one investigation in which doctors were presented with identical symptoms from male and female patients. The doctors were much more likely to diagnose the women as suffering from psychosomatic complaints whereas the men were thought to have "real" problems. Women are twice as likely to be identified as suffering from neurotic emotional problems, and they make up more than two-thirds of those who seek the services of therapists. Interestingly, this is not necessarily because of greater emotional instability, but the result of a tendency to show more what they are feeling. Our culture, traditionally dominated by patriarchal norms, does not value the female qualities of emotional expressiveness. Such behavior is labeled as hysterical and neurotic. And whereas our society puts a premium on emotional restraint, this does not necessarily indicate a healthy strategy.

Since women have been socially conditioned not to react aggressively when they feel fearful or hurt, this frustration is more often expressed as tears. Crying, however, is not simply misplaced aggression, nor is it anger turned inward; it is the statement by someone of the depth and strength of the feelings. It is a sincere plea for understanding.

Really Talking

Feminist scholars like Mary Belenky write about distinctly women's ways of relating to the world. She describes the typically male way of communicating as "didactic talking" in which people "hold forth" rather than share ideas with one another. The object of such an exchange is to present oneself in the best possible light, to explain, enlighten, persuade, influence, cajole. "Really talking," by contrast, involves a deep level of mutual sharing in which both participants feel listened to and understood. They help one another to explore ideas, to build on them and make them grow. This, of course, is what therapy is all about—an experience so rare that people are willing to pay lots of money for the privilege.

Even in the use of verbal language, differences between genders are significant. When men use the pronoun *we,* they often mean the exclusionary "us versus them," as in "*We* are right and *they* are wrong." Women, on the other hand, usually use *we* to mean "all of us together," creating connections and intimacy between people.

Just as a woman's voice of self-expression is different

from a man's, so too are her tears. One businesswoman describes the plight of curtailing her emotional nature in a male-dominated world, where the consequences of showing emotion are disastrous.

> When I cry, my mental abilities don't stop, even though it might look that way to some people. I am looking for a way to explain how I feel, but at that moment no words come out. I'm tied up in knots.

> The more I fight the impulse to cry, the more likely the tears will come. I know that as soon as I start I will be dismissed immediately, especially by men. I lose all credibility.

> When I cry, it means I've failed with words. I am out of control, just a weak, helpless, vulnerable woman who is incapable of expressing herself.

In her book *The Managed Heart,* Arlie Hochschild explains that in the absence of other options "women make a resource out of feeling and offer it to men as a gift in return for the more material resources they lack." As offensive as this sounds, she cites the economic disadvantages women have suffered throughout history. Even today in our supposedly enlightened era of gender equality, men are generally paid more than women for identical contributions.

Consequently, Hochschild describes feeling as the primary *work* of women. They are the emotional caretakers and managers of relationships. As every marital therapist well knows, the vast majority of times that new couples call for initial appointments, it is the woman who is making the contact. Since the majority of clients who seek counseling are female, it is also clear that many are attending sessions on behalf of their husbands, boyfriends, sons, and fathers.

In recent research conducted on what makes for successful marriages, one of the factors most often noted is the wife's investment in being the emotional caretaker. Once she gets sick and tired of always being the one to initiate conversation, to move the relationship to a deeper level, the marriage may end.

Really talking involves the best part of both men and women. It requires a degree of listening and cooperation, responding from the heart, a feeling of safety to think or cry, to take risks with one another in the path toward intimacy and mutual understanding. Yet the attributes of analytic inquiry and passionate debate, traditionally within the male domain, are also important in making sense of what is taking place and moving conversation along to new levels.

The genders represent polarities between reasoning and intuition, thinking and feeling, the head and the heart. Crying transcends all other human experience. It integrates the cerebral cortex, that master of logic, with the limbic system, that seat of emotion, into a human response that is all encompassing.

Crying is a language of really talking, not merely reporting your perceptions and experience. It represents not only an attempt to say something but a plea for a particular response that involves both the head and the heart. Exactly how these responses are elicited depends mostly on socialization processes that take place within particular cultural contexts, as we discussed in the previous chapter.

WHY WOMEN CRY

There is the age-old debate as to which is the most significant determinant of human behavior—genetics or environment. Do women cry more than men because they are biologically better equipped to do so, or because they are trained from an early age to express feelings while men are taught to repress them?

Surely it is obvious to the most passionate proponent of either position that both culture and Nature have a hand in shaping women to be such fluent criers.

A Cross-Cultural View

In most cultures throughout the world, women tend to internalize their feelings while men are more likely to externalize them. Women are more prone to experience the full brunt of their losses and to express them through tears. Men access their anger more readily. At the extreme, women learn helplessness while men learn violence.

In the Andaman Islands near Burma, for example, women sit around and grieve through their tears while the men scream fierce curses at the spirits, shooting arrows in all directions to express their anger. Among the Cubeo Indians of the Amazon, a similar contrasting style is evident. The grieving widow of the deceased, and other women of the village, caress the corpse and weep freely. The men load their weapons and stand in a circle around the body. Screaming threats of retaliation against real or imagined enemies, they then fire their weapons in the air. This, of course, is how wars begin.

Looking further at cultural influences on gender differences, we see that women often attain status based on how well they cry while men do so by proving how well they can restrain their tears. In the Philippines, Roy Barton noted dramatic distinctions among the Ifugaos: "A female relative, on first arriving at the death chair, will always wail, usually with her blanket over her head, and this wailing will probably be joined in by other female relatives that are present. Sometimes the women scratch their faces so that they run with blood. . . . Men do not wail, but they sometimes chop their heads or slash their bodies with bolos, especially if it be a child of theirs who died."

In various parts of Africa or the South Pacific, or among native peoples of our own continent, the more copiously a woman cries, the more dramatically she wails, the better able she is to win sympathy and prove her love for the deceased. By contrast, men in these cultures, as in our own, demonstrate their fortitude through holding back any displays of emotion.

Biological Determinants

Cultural conditioning alone does not account for the often vast gulf between the genders in terms of how they react emotionally. There are very real biological differences as well, especially with regard to physiology, endocrine functions, and brain chemistry.

New technologies such as functional magnetic resonance imagery and positron emission tomography have allowed researchers to observe electrochemical and temperature changes in the brain during various tasks such as solving math problems or recognizing emotional cues. In a series of studies on sex differences that were motivated by their own temperamental anomalies, the husband-wife team of Bennett and Sally Shaywitz found that whereas both men and women are able to recognize happiness when they see it, sadness presents a different challenge. Women are able to identify sadness on people's faces about 90 percent of the time. Interestingly, men can do equally well in reading other men's faces but are only 70 percent accurate in recognizing sadness in women. This is explained by evolutionary theory as the result of greater necessity for men to be able to anticipate reactions of competitors than to read the responses of their mates.

This difference in performance is hardly surprising, of course, since women have been complaining for centuries that men are emotionally insensitive to their needs and unwilling (unable?) to tell when they are feeling blue, and not capable of interpreting their language of tears. What has been revealed by these new neurological studies, however, is that there seem to be distinct biological differences between the genders in the anatomy and physiology of their brains.

For example, women have more volume in the corpus callosum—the bridge between the two cerebral hemispheres—which makes communication and language easier. When women are making sense of emotional reactions, their limbic systems are less active than those of men engaged in the same tasks. In other words, men's brains have to work much harder when decoding emotional responses.

On the other hand, when people are asked to recall tearful memories, the limbic system is activated eight times as much in women than men. This may offer a compelling reason why women are much more susceptible to depression and far more likely to cry.

We may conclude from this recent flurry of neurobiological evidence that gender differences in emotional experiences and expression may very well be determined by our brains as well as by our cultural upbringing. It is harder for men to cry, as well as to respond to others' tears, because they are underequipped to do so. Just as men's brains function better for the language of quantitative tasks or aggressive behavior, the language of tears and its underlying emotional sensitivity falls within the province of female neurological strengths.

There are not only differences in brain chemistry that predispose men to do anger and women to do tears, but also differences in hormonal levels. Just as men are known to have higher concentrations of testosterone, which are associated with explosive anger and hostility, so too do women's higher levels of prolactin, the hormone that is necessary for milk production, account for greater tear stimulation. As we explored in Chapter Three, women have a higher need to excrete excess prolactin, which can possibly do the body harm in higher doses. Aside from breast-feeding, one of the most direct ways to accomplish this task is to cry. Further confirming this theory, older women do not cry nearly as often and are even prone to a condition called *dry eye syndrome* because they are not producing enough tears once they hit menopause and prolactin production stops.

It is also well known that the menstrual cycle plays a role in reducing the threshold for tears at certain times of the month. Some studies have indicated that the frequency of women's crying during this period increases five times!

These biological differences are compounded as they become manifest in daily life. Just ask yourself what women most value when compared to men. One fundamental distinction, consistent with our biological imperatives, is that females are more relationship oriented while males are more concerned with aspects of productivity. Men care about goals; women care more about process. Men are known to be more competitive while women function more cooperatively. In each of these cases, crying is the language that is most useful for people interested in communicating within cooperative, process-oriented relationships. That is why tears fall primarily within the sphere of female experience.

For example, two highly competitive professionals, one a male football coach, the other a female basketball coach, both discuss their volatile reactions to learning that one of their team members was involved in a drug scandal. The male coach reports that his first reactions were of betrayal and anger: "How could he let me down like that! How could he let the team down!" This more measured reaction had been preceded by an emotional tirade of spectacular proportions, sending staff members scurrying for cover.

Faced with identical circumstances, the female coach's first reaction was one of hurt. With tears in her eyes, she spoke of her own disappointment, but also of her concern for the athlete whose life was going down the tubes. Both of these coaches are in very competitive fields; their very jobs are in jeopardy as a result of these scandals. Yet, their emotional reactions to the situation are very much determined by their biological predispositions. It is not that one response is necessarily more effective than the other; each communicates disappointment in a different style, a manner that has been, at least historically, distinctly male or female. In the last few decades, however, gender roles are becoming more and more confusing.

THE TWO WORLDS OF PROFESSIONAL WOMEN

As men become more emotionally expressive and women take on more traditional masculine roles as breadwinners, heads of household, chief executive officers, or fighter pilots, a blending of gender roles is taking place. *Androgyny* refers to the best parts of masculine and feminine traits—the person who is both strong and sensitive, assertive and empathic, courageous and vulnerable.

In their efforts to win acceptance and respect in a world of male-dominated values, many professional women who have entered the work world as surgeons, engineers, lawyers, and politicians have often abandoned stereotypical female traits, including the ability to cry. One female physician describes this as a kind of castration of her femininity:

Medical school destroyed whatever soft part of me I held dear. In order to succeed, more than that, in order to excel as one of the few women around, I had to act like a man.

I will never forget during a third year rotation when I was sent in to take the vital signs of a cancer patient. I saw her lying in bed, bald, emaciated, tubes running in and out of her, and I just felt so sorry for her. After I took her blood pressure, I kept her hand in mine and we just cried together. It was so moving . . . until the resident burst in and demanded to know what the hell was going on: "And you want to be a doctor?" he said sarcastically. "If you are going to pull shit like this, why don't you just be a nurse!"

That was the last time I cried openly for a patient. In fact, now that I think about it, I don't hardly cry at all any more.

The price women pay for thriving in male-dominated professions has been to sacrifice their essential femaleness. They wear suits in imitation of men's wardrobe, complete with ties. They adopt traditionally male communication styles in which the emphasis is on goals rather than process. They have given away their tears in lieu of more aggressive male traits that serve them better in the workplace.

Whereas in early adolescence girls were told that crying would hardly compromise their status in others' eyes, and many times would even accrue the benefits of being rescued, as adults many were forced to learn a more masculine sex role that is predominant in the corporate world. When you have been humiliated or attacked or disappointed or saddened by something that just occurred in a staff meeting, you may feel like crying, but breaking out into tears is not a viable option if you intend to keep your job.

At Home

Cassie is the mother of two elementary school children and the wife of a building contractor. She considers herself quite dedicated to both of these traditional female roles. She enjoys taking care of her loved ones, and especially appreciates the beginning of the day as she launches her family into the world. This particular morning Cassie enters her daughters' room to wake them up, only to discover the remnants of a disaster that occurred the previous night. Apparently, the girls had decided to redecorate their room with splendid crayon drawings on the walls. As she stood stunned, trying to figure out how they had managed to get splashes of color on the ceiling, she also noticed that even the door had been mutilated by some artistic vision that escaped her. Cassie's shock, confusion, frustration, anger, and disappointment loomed so big in her heart, tears began to spill down her cheeks.

By the time she had gathered herself together enough to wake the girls and find out what happened, Cassie's husband now entered the scene. How could she have allowed the children to remain unsupervised the previous night while he worked late, Cassie's husband wondered? Oh, so now this was *her* fault? Right.

Cassie stormed out of the room, once again in tears, and locked herself in the bathroom to regain her composure. She would be late for work unless she hurried. Still, she took an extra moment or two to stare at her reflection in the mirror. She watched the remnants of tears drying on her cheek as if they were some strange substance belonging to someone else. In a way, these tears did come from someone else's eyes.

At Work

In addition to being a wife and mother, Cassie also works in a predominately masculine world. She is the principal litigator for a prestigious law firm. In fact, she is one of only three female attorneys in the building and the only one with the status of partner. Furthermore, she has chosen the ultimate arena of masculine aggression as her specialty—the combat of trial law.

This same woman, who hours earlier cried in frustration and helplessness in her feminine roles as wife and mother, was now listening alertly and grimly as a few of her colleagues challenged the way she handled a case. Just as with her daughters, she felt ambushed. Just as with her husband, she felt unfairly blamed. This time, however, there was not only coldness in her eyes but steel in her heart. If you had interrupted Cassie at this moment and asked her what she was feeling inside, this woman who at home is so expressive of her emotions would look at you with faint amusement and a stare that has been known to give even judges chills down their spines. "Why, I feel nothing at all," she would truthfully reply.

Like so many women who must operate in a setting dominated by masculine values of power and control, Cassie straddles the worlds of both genders. By day, the thought that she would display any emotions except those calculated to elicit a particular advantage in her arguments is inconceivable. Yet, when she is at home some switch in her brain permits her a freedom of emotional expression, including a fluency in the language of tears, that is quite a contrast with her predatory style in the courtroom.

> At first, this difference between my two selves used to bother me quite a lot. I noticed the changes as soon as I began law school. I had this real jealous boyfriend at the time and he used to expect me to be fairly compliant. He liked it when I was tearful and emotional; then he felt more in control. In all honesty, I didn't mind either. I liked him taking care of me.
>
> Then, when I was at school, I was this cutthroat, competitive bitch. Really, I wasn't a bitch—I just acted the way a successful guy would act. I was real aggressive and hard.
>
> Yet, when I came home I felt soft again. I have always felt free to cry when I am home, but I wouldn't dream of doing so in my other life.

Cassie keeps her two worlds separate, and does so in a way that she is able to maintain both lives. At work she communicates like the ultimate macho warrior; at home, she speaks in the language of tears.

According to those who have studied women's transitions in the workplace, Cassie's split style of feminine/masculine emotional expression is not unusual. Women are socialized primarily in the nuances of intimacy in relationships. In the work world, and especially in the arena of corporations and law firms, the predominant values are the antithesis of those for which women have been prepared. The organizational structures are bureaucratic, impersonal, and authoritarian. They value aggression, ambition, power, single-minded devotion to productivity over relationships, and goals over process. Crying in these circumstances is out of the question.

How Women Bridge the Gap

I'm a crier. I tell guys that when I first start dating them. I want them to understand that when I cry they don't have to overreact or anything. Just accept me. Still, I chase them away. They get angry or frustrated with me. They think I am trying to manipulate them or something. Why don't men realize that tears don't have to be such a big deal?

Why indeed? As this woman, Adrian, laments how her tears consistently create problems in her relationships, she wonders why this language presents such a barrier between the genders. If there is a single emotional difference that parallels anatomical contrasts between men and women, it is the expression of feeling through tears. Adrian cries freely and without shame in a variety of circumstances. She likes this about herself even if she has yet to meet any men who are willing to tolerate, much less appreciate, her tearful nature.

Frustrated and confused about these conflicts, Adrian, or any woman who finds herself in a similar situation, would be well advised to consider the following questions:

What do your tears mean to a man that is different from what they mean to you? It happens that people bring their previous experiences to any current situation. When someone has felt used or manipulated in the past, he is inclined to be suspicious in the future under similar circumstances. In fact, for every story a woman has to tell about how she was treated insensitively during a crying episode, there is a comparable anecdote of a man who felt himself to have been victimized by manipulative tears. Keep in mind that roughly half of all women would be willing to cry deliberately or show emotion to get their way, whereas only 20 percent of men would be willing to do so.

What are you really in dispute about? In any tearful conflict it is extremely important to talk together openly about which needs are not being met, to speak without assigning blame or guilt as to who is mostly at fault, and to explore together how the present disagreement is related to struggles in the past that are being reenacted.

In other words, ask yourself what you are really in disagreement about. Rather than focusing on the tears themselves, or even the underlying emotions alone, consider the larger picture. When men and women are speaking different languages of tears, unable to find common ground, it may be because they have failed to recognize and address the real issues between them.

How has trust been breached? Can I believe that what you are expressing is heartfelt and genuine? Can I trust you to be open and honest? In order to feel comfortable crying—a state of extreme vulnerability—it's critical that there be high levels of trust. While this seems fairly obvious to women, many men must be taught this important principle.

In Adrian's case, she actually made an effort to sit her current lover down and explain that to her the single most important part of a relationship was feeling safe. If that couldn't be established, then being able to cry freely was the least of her problems. If it doesn't feel safe for you to cry in any of your closest relationships, you may have to consider the inevitable but uncomfortable conclusion—that you don't fully trust these people.

How can you help the feelings behind the tears to speak in other ways? Crying is a beginning but not the end point of deep communication. Before the other person shuts down in frustration, or flees in exasperation, at least communicate that it is difficult to talk just then. Ask for what you need in the meantime before you can put your feelings into words.

How are issues of power coming into play? We have seen elsewhere how tears can be used manipulatively to equalize power in relationships in which one party feels overwhelmed. Genuine tears also occur during those times when a woman feels overwhelmed, misunderstood, or exploited.

What is interesting to explore as well is how the man also feels powerless. We have seen how he is more likely to express those feelings in angry rather than crying behavior.

Nonetheless, each of us feels powerless, individually as well as collectively, during tearful misunderstandings. Each person is seeking more control over the other.

What are you saying to one another right now? There is an exercise that marital therapists are quite fond of employing during times in a session when a couple is neither hearing accurately nor responding appropriately. Each partner is required to repeat back to the other's satisfaction exactly what he or she heard the person say, before he or she is allowed to continue. This means that before things escalate to the point where each person feels misunderstood, both partners would have to work very hard to decode accurately just what the tears or other verbal expressions are saying. Before Adrian's boyfriend becomes angry, or feels guilty or frustrated or manipulated, he would tease out expressed messages in the manner of a gentle and caring investigator:

> So you are feeling bad just now, really bad. . . . No? . . . You are shaking your head no. . . . Okay. Help me then. You're not so much feeling bad as you are disappointed. You are disappointed in something I did? There's more? Okay, you also want me not to push you so much to talk just yet, just let the tears flow.

Likewise, Adrian would apply the same strategy of identifying first what she heard before she responds:

> You're feeling like I'm blaming you unfairly for something you don't even know you did. You wish I'd stop all this crying and just say what I want.

Once any two people speaking different languages take the time and patience to learn one another's vocabulary, to help one another feel understood, to reach out in a way that communicates openness, the interaction will more likely prove satisfying, even across the gender divide.

The language of tears has traditionally been the specialty of women, a trend that is changing as they take on more of the responsibilities and roles that have previously been assigned to men. With greater authority and responsibility come different expectations for what is considered appropriate emotional displays. In the next chapter, we continue our discussion of these unique dialects by concentrating on the experience of men.

7

when men cry

Men speak a different language of tears, no less poignant and meaningful than that of women. What they lack in apparent frequency, fluency, and intensity of tears, they more than make up for in unique richness and complexity.

Time and time again, men have been accused of lacking emotional depth, if not the ability to express themselves fully. In reality, it's not that men don't speak through their tears, but rather that their language is not often acknowledged or validated. This feeling is not unlike what many women feel when they must conform to a predominately masculine ideal of what is considered competent.

Women enjoy special advantages in the world of communication, both biologically—in terms of greater innate talent in this arena—and culturally—in that they are specifically trained to be sensitive to nuances of feeling. Men, on the other hand, have been told since they were first able to understand language that if they are going to make it this world they must do it by hiding what they really feel.

THE LANGUAGE OF MEN'S TEARS

Men do express themselves through tears, even if their communications are often ignored, unappreciated, or misunderstood. One reason for this is that men's strongest and deepest expressions of tears are not necessarily of pain, but of empathy, pride, and joy. Once you apply an appropriate framework for understanding the unique language that expresses uniquely masculine values, men are found to be remarkably articulate in their feelings.

I am not just speaking about the so-called postmodern, sensitive man either, the yuppie professional guy who participates in male bonding sweat lodges, eats sushi, and has done a lengthy stint in therapy. Almost all men have within them the capacity to speak deeply through their tears, if only people know how to hear them.

When Men Are Moved

Four guys are sitting around a table, drinking beer, talking about their lives. They are overheard presenting their respective opinions about why the local college football team lost its last game. They rattle around politics for awhile, making fun of the candidates in the next election, finding each one comical and unacceptable. But their laughter ends abruptly as one of the men begins telling his friends about the feelings he had watching his son play tennis in a state tournament.

> I couldn't believe the way my little guy was so self-assured and composed out there. I was so proud of the way he handled

himself. I didn't care if he won the match or not—I just couldn't believe what class he showed.

Tears came to the man's eyes as his voice choked with feeling. His friends were utterly still, riveted by his story, their attention split between what they had just heard and what they were feeling in sympathy while they related to this experience in their own personal ways.

One of the men reached over and affectionately punched his friend on the arm. To an untrained observer, it would appear as if he was making light of the story and was sloughing it off, anxious to move away from the terrain of tears and back to the familiar ground of politics and football.

Make no mistake, however. He was *profoundly* moved by what he just heard. Even more so, the presence of his friend's tears spoke to him in a way that led him to feel like crying as well. In fact, to anyone who looked at him very closely, it would be apparent that he *was* crying even though no sobs could be heard, nor could more than a little extra moisture be detected along the bottom of his eyelids. If you looked further, you would see the fingernails of his left hand digging into his palm, his eyes blinking rapidly, and his breathing accelerated both in depth and pitch. This man had been moved, after all, not only by his friend's story but by feelings of regret that he did not have children of his own and would never know what it felt like to look with pride on a son or daughter.

Here is a man who is crying, perhaps not technically, as no actual tears escaped his lids, but on the verge. Likewise, if you looked around the table, another of the men was crying in sympathy as well. Again tears were not actually visible, but if you looked closely at his trembling lip and nervous foot, or better yet, got inside his head and heart, you would feel the intensity of his reaction.

So, what is it about this episode of restrained tears that qualifies for being included in our discussion? How can this be called crying when none of the usual symptoms are present? The answers to these and other questions about the ways that men are moved and express their feelings are found in the unique ways they communicate.

What Are the Differences?

Forms of self-expression can be both obvious and subtle, flamboyant and restrained. One of the reasons that men's tears have gone unacknowledged is because they don't conform to the usual standards we have come to expect from the more dramatic demonstrations of crying that are more characteristic of women.

Specifically related to the distinct language of tears spoken by men, the following features are most evident:

Men are less inclined to use tears manipulatively. This is true for the simple reason that such a strategy wouldn't work. Whereas it is easy to imagine instances in which a woman might resort to tears as a way to improve her leverage, a man crying during negotiations would only elicit feelings of disdain and disrespect. More often, when a man cries it is because something really authentic is going on.

Men cry in more subtle ways. They cry less often, for shorter duration, and shed fewer tears. They make less noise and draw less attention to themselves. In many cases, they even hide their faces when they are crying so as to minimize the literal loss of face.

Whereas until puberty boys and girls cry just about as often, even if there are different triggers for these emotional events, there is a dramatic change at about the time boys are expected to adopt the more traditional values of male adults. Several surveys have confirmed quantitatively what you instinctively know to be true, even if you would be surprised by the extent of the gender difference: about 80 percent of men report that they never cry, or hardly ever, as compared to a similar percentage of women who do cry on a regular basis. For those men who do admit to crying, only 15 percent sob and shake during their episodes, compared to 65 percent of women. The vast majority of the time (61 percent), crying for men means simply having red eyes and shedding a tear or two.

Men tend to cry in response to specific situations. A study led by William Lombardo found that men are likely to cry in response to only two situations that are equivalent to those for women—the death of a loved one and a moving religious experience. Other than that, while 20 percent of women admit to crying when they are frightened, men almost never cry under those circumstances. Likewise, men are eight times less likely than women to cry when they are being yelled at and nine times less likely to cry at sentimental gatherings like weddings.

Male tears tend to be most uniquely expressive in those situations for which men were designed to function: in combat, either in the battlefield or in simulated conditions. Thus, crying for fallen comrades is especially within the male province, as is crying in defeat when the spoils of commercial or social wars become unattainable.

Men look more toward internal rather than external cues when they cry. The male nervous system seems to process information a bit differently from the way things work for women. This means that male tears arise from altogether different cues, especially those that are internally rather than externally based. Whereas women look more at external cues in the environment and social interactions, men are more inclined to tune into their bodies. For example, whereas a woman may cry in response to what is being said or done to her, a man is more likely to shed tears as a result of what he is experiencing in his body as a response to what happens in the outside world. First, he watches his child being born. Then he notices that his heart is racing, his stomach feels fluttery, his throat constricted. *Then* his tears start to flow. The process often requires one more step between an activating event and the subsequent tears.

Men cry most uniquely in response to feelings that are part of their core identity. Just as women are most fluent crying in response to themes of attachment and loss, men specialize in tears related to their basic nature, however much they are conditioned to hold these feelings in check.

Men have a unique identity, one that is framed in most cultures in the roles of provider, protector, warrior, athlete, husband, father, and team player. There are particular feelings associated with each of these assigned or adopted roles—male tears are more inclined to express felt experiences of pride, bravery, loyalty, victory, and defeat.

A man cries as he hears himself warn his child to be careful as she leaves the house. Why? Because he remembers his father saying the exact same thing to him in the same way. A man is praised by a colleague at work, sparking an unexpected torrent of tears. Why? Because he is deeply appreciative that his extra efforts had been noticed by someone; he is not used to being acknowledged by other men. A baseball player sits in the dugout and cries for fifteen minutes after his team has lost the World Series. Why? To express his deep feelings of disappointment at trying his best and it still wasn't enough. In each of these instances, men are crying in ways that are often different from those in which women might be most moved.

Men are not inclined to explain their tears. They are not only less willing to do so but they are far less motivated than women to talk things through. It is as if the tears speak for themselves. Talking about them just diminishes their meaning and power. Men prefer instead an action mode, one that leads to taking care of what is bothersome, or at least putting things far enough behind that normal business can resume.

While our culture labels such behavior as restrictive, insensitive, inarticulate, and words with similarly negative connotations, most of these judgments are made within a largely feminine definition of communication, which is espoused by most social scientists and mental health professionals. That is one reason that accounts for the disproportionately small number of men who agree to participate in therapy, and for the way those who do are more likely than women to drop out prematurely. The task of therapy is one in which participants are asked—no, demanded—to acknowledge and express feelings in particular ways. Oftentimes, this task is inconsistent with what men have been taught all their lives to do.

Men work hard to suppress and curtail their tears. Men cry an average of two minutes per episode, as compared to six minutes for women. One reason that men cry less often and for shorter duration is that they have learned to stop their tears from flowing. Through some fairly traumatic lessons in life, men have come to value their ability to regain control of themselves even under the most adverse conditions. To not have developed this skill of cutting off tears would subject the male to vicious name-calling as a crybaby, wimp, or mama's boy.

Men apologize for their tears. Not having been rewarded very often for crying, since such behavior represented a humiliating loss of control, men are likely to feel remorse and shame after letting their tears show. Rather than feeling good about their authentic expressions of self, or even relieved at the release of tension, they more often feel some degree of regret and resolve to show more self-control in the future. The result of this self-restraint is that the average man cries only once per month, roughly one quarter as often as women.

Men show more variation in their crying, depending on their particular peer group. Education level, social class, sexual orientation, and identification with a stereotypical masculine sex role are all factors that influence the likelihood of men's fluency in the language of tears. The various subcultures of maleness have quite different rules for how and when tears may be expressed. Among our group of four men sitting at the table, for instance, a few drops of moisture are considered acceptable, but anything more dramatic would be deemed unseemly. Those who tend to be more educated, more flexible in the ways they define themselves as men, are likely to cry more often and in more varied circumstances.

Men's tears are more potent. It is because crying is a relatively rare event in a man's life that when he does speak through his tears, people are inclined to pay attention. Men's tears often make other people uncomfortable as well, whereas when women cry, it could mean a major catastrophe or, on the other hand, be seen as an overreaction to something relatively insignificant. When a man cries, you *know* it is serious. It takes an awful lot to get male tears flowing, and if they are present, they will communicate a powerful message.

How Men React to Tears

Men not only speak differently through their tears, they also respond to crying in ways that are often misunderstood. In the following interaction, which took place in a counseling group for high-functioning individuals, the characteristic style with which the men reacted to the tears of the women is particularly instructive of the differences that are manifest.

Teachers and therapists themselves, the group members were meeting together for support mostly, but also to engage one another on an intimate level. They wanted to hear the truth. They wanted to know how they were perceived by others. They wanted to complete their unfinished business of the past.

A man began speaking first, in a voice that was deep, resonant, authoritative. He was admonishing his peers about something, and they appeared defensive. Feet began tapping a nervous rhythm. Eyes stared intently at the floor. Knees moved further apart. Two lips trembled.

As he continued chastising them for playing it safe, for

avoiding authentic risk taking, settling for predictable mediocrity in the ways they related to one another, the quivering lips of one woman spread across her face, beginning a chain reaction. Her eyes squeezed shut, tensing the rest of the muscles in her face. Her body closed in on itself, arms embracing her knees. Breathing accelerated, muting the sounds that occasionally escaped her rubbery lips. Tears trickled from her eyes, down her cheeks, creating tiny puddles in her lap.

There was an instantaneous reaction in the group. A box of tissue was passed to her as quickly as the most poised nurse would hand off a sponge to a surgeon. The man stopped his speech in midsentence. All eyes were now riveted on the woman, waiting for some explanation as to what she was experiencing. What sparked this reaction? What is she feeling? What is she saying by her behavior?

Haltingly, through hiccups, breathless words, sometimes soundless lips forming phrases that were never launched, the woman explained herself. She described what her tears meant. She identified the trigger that set her off: the feeling that she was being attacked. She described what that was like for her, what it reminded her of. A chorus of other women jumped in to lend support, echoing that they too often felt their tears were misunderstood.

The man now became defensive, even angry. He felt responsible, guilty, the perpetrator of a crime. Yet he also felt like a victim, as if he had been betrayed:

Wait a minute. Just one minute! Is it my imagination or did we just change the whole focus of this discussion because you began crying? It seems like we were onto something important. It touched you. It frightened you. I didn't hurt you; at least I didn't *mean* to. Why do I feel like such a monster right now, as if I made you cry?

Everyone jumped in now. They all had something to say about the part of this conversation that spoke to them. The women accused the men of being unfeeling and insensitive; the men responded with their own accusations that tears have lost their deeper meaning because they are so diluted by women who use them for manipulation. They worked at sorting out who was most misunderstood. They tried to make sense of the sequence of events. They began to translate the language of tears, deciphering its syntax and grammar, dissecting its vocabulary, its power and poetry.

Another man in the group talked about his own reactions to the proceedings: "I hate it when women cry. It always feels like I did something bad. I made it happen. It is all my fault. I close down after that."

He was interrupted by another: "I disagree. We are certainly discouraged from crying. It is not manly. It is weak. Vulnerable. But. . . ."

The tearful woman raised her voice above the fray, asserting herself in a way they had never seen before. "You just don't understand, not any of you! You all make assumptions about what tears mean, as if they always say the same thing. I cry for so many reasons—when I am hurt or frustrated, sure, but also when I feel moved."

The preceding discussion typifies clearly the ways that men react differently from women to the presence of tears.

The man felt angry rather than compassionate toward the tearful woman, not because he was necessarily insensitive or unfeeling but because he interpreted very different meaning in her behavior than was seen by the other women. We have discussed in the previous chapter some of the reasons to account for these different perceptual filters. One inescapable conclusion that we can now reach is that we are not speaking, in fact, about *the* language of tears but of many languages that are spoken by different cultures and both genders.

A DOUBLE STANDARD

Scoff all you like at the emotional restriction of men who seem unwilling or unable to cry, but the consequences they face for doing so are far more serious than for women. There is, in fact, a double standard operating, the same one that judges women harshly for expressing their anger.

In a survey of twenty thousand young people completed in 1978, three-quarters of the girls and two-thirds of the boys thought it was all right for women to cry publicly, but only 58 percent of the girls and 42 percent of the boys believed this was acceptable in men. In a study of college-age students that duplicated this original *Scholastic Magazine* questionnaire, Gary Crester and his co-researchers found that an interesting double standard emerged on the part of male respondents. Men hold a much more rigid, stereotypical view of sex roles in general and of crying in particular. Whereas many women feel sympathetic and accepting toward men who cry in certain circumstances, the same is definitely not the case with men toward others of their gender. Men see women crying as generally neutral, or even positive, but view other men doing so as inappropriate and a clear sign of weakness.

These differences are evident in other areas as well. In cry perception studies, adults were asked to listen to various infant cries and to interpret what they might mean by rating them on several scales. With respect to gender differences, men more often than women perceive irritation and anger in infant crying. In addition, they are more likely to perceive difficult crying as indicative of being spoiled, meaning that they would be less inclined to offer comfort. Mothers are also less disturbed than fathers by the crying of their own children. The results of these studies suggest that not only are men less sensitive but they also experience more internal disruption when they hear crying, a circumstance that results in part from indoctrination into their particular sex role.

Male Conditioning

The differences between men and women in the ways they cry are most easily understood in terms of traditional sex roles, in how they are taught to respond to various situations. During times of sadness, for example, girls are encouraged to talk about their feelings, to cry, to support one another through touch and compassionate listening. Boys, on the other hand, are told not to sit around and mope, most definitely not to cry like a baby, but to express themselves through productive work or aggression.

In another example of facing a distressing situation such as a baby crying, traditional women—and men who have adopted a more flexible sex role—will respond compassionately and sensitively to the infant. However, men who may be described as traditionally masculine in their values are likely to become angry rather than empathic.

Think about the different messages boys and girls receive growing up. Boys are told they are acting like babies, or worse, that they are acting like girls when they cry. Yet girls are actually encouraged to cry as a legitimate means to express themselves. As a champion of the men's movement, Warren Farrell explains one of the reasons that men grow up so emotionally conflicted and restricted is because of the ways they are indoctrinated with mixed messages:

- Be strong, yet sensitive.
- Be powerful, yet conciliatory.
- Be expressive, yet not overly emotional.
- Be vulnerable, yet not tearful.

Perhaps the most paradoxical message of all is the one that comes primarily from women: be sensitive, yet successful. In other words, what women want from men is someone who is kind, caring, loving, and vulnerable. Yet they also want someone who is successful, who has prestige, power, or money. What it takes to be successful are exactly the opposite qualities from the ones involved in being caring—you must be aggressive, suspicious, controlling, ambitious, driven, and self-involved. Therefore, the messages that men receive are that they should be vulnerable and emotionally expressive at home, but they should also do what it takes at work to get ahead.

In a series of interviews with women about their reactions to men who cry, Cindy Chupack found some very mixed messages. Women say they like a sensitive guy who can express his feelings through tears—but only at funerals and weddings. In the words of one woman: "I like a man who's not afraid to cry . . . but *doesn't*."

It is no wonder that men are increasingly confused about whether to cry or not. Speaking for many others, one man describes his predicament:

> I have only recently learned to cry again. It started a few years ago when my wife and I were having some trouble. She used to beg me to show some emotion but, hey, I'm an accountant. I use my brain all day putting numbers in proper places. There is no place for emotion in my work. In order to make partner, you have to be more ruthless than any of the other associates, more willing to do what it takes to get a job done. If I cried at work I would be history. If I showed any feeling at all, it would be exploited in some way.
>
> Then I come home and all of a sudden the rules change. I am supposed to walk through the door, let my accountant-self go, and immediately slip into the role of caring dad and husband. I've got to tell you, sometimes I do get confused. Since I am trying so hard to reveal more of myself to my wife and kids, the other day I was talking to my secretary at work, listening to her story about her mother dying of cancer, and tears came to my eyes. I know she saw them and was shocked! We just don't do that sort of thing, so I quickly recovered and pretended like I had something caught in my eye.

In a book about why boys don't cry, educators Sue Askew and Carol Ross describe the socialization process by which images of masculinity are constructed in such a way as to discourage emotional expression. We would only have to listen in at any gathering of parents and toddlers to hear the nicknames reserved for each gender, already reinforcing traditional norms. "Thus, little girls are called 'honey,' 'sweetie pie,' 'cutie,' 'love,' 'precious,' 'darling,' while boys are called affectionately 'trouble,' 'buster,' and 'bruiser.'" What are little girls made of? Why, sugar and spice, and everything nice. And boys? Why naturally, puppy dogs' tails.

Masculine Tears

It was all very confusing for me as a boy. My father sometimes would spank me, hit me *hard*. Even worse is that he would forbid me to cry. "Cry and I'll only make it tougher for you!" he would tell me.

So here is this big guy whaling on me. I'm scared and angry and really hurting. I want to cry. Bad. But if I do, I get it worse. It was not being able to cry that hurt worse than the beatings.

I wish I could say that this man's story was unusual, that his experience is relatively rare. Unfortunately, so many men tell similar tales of how their tears were beaten out of them when they were youngsters, and how as adults they had to learn to cry once again. This process is illustrated through the narrative of another man:

As a young boy, whenever I cried my father would make fun of me. He called me a sissy, said I wasn't really his son. What kind of man would I be if I was such a wimp?

I couldn't have been more than six or seven at the time. It used to upset me whenever my mother would leave for awhile, leaving me with people I didn't know. I remember crying during those times, after which my father would tell me to hush up, even threaten me with dire consequences if I continued.

I stopped crying for thirty years after those days—ironically, until my father died. It was as if by crying for him I was free to shed my own tears once again.

There is a myth that men don't cry, and when they do break down, says TV producer Stuart Cosgrove, "it is seen as an event of such profound significance that it begs attention and floods the onlooker with a belief that something important has taken place." From his perspective through a camera's eye, Cosgrove has witnessed more than his fair share of masculine weeping, usually in the context of that familiar scenario when an athlete cries over winning the big game, as if that is the only thing that could move a man to tears.

A man's tears are considered so rare and powerful that they have been known to sway public opinion, even a whole political election. In what was to become only the first in a series of scandals that marked his professional life, Richard Nixon was about to be dropped from the 1952 presidential ticket after it was discovered he had been on the payroll of wealthy businessmen while a senator from California. During his famous speech to save the day, Nixon shed a tear as he confessed that he was so poor that all he had to his name was a cloth coat and his dog Checkers. Adlai Stevenson was absolutely incensed that his opponent would resort to sympathetic tears, claiming that anyone who would cry deserved to lose. That miscalculation helped to lose the election for Stevenson.

Tracing the tradition of male tears to manipulate in what has been thought of as a traditionally feminine strategy, Philip Dunne cites several other examples of what he calls "political lachrymosity." In a chilling reenactment of Nixon's "Check-ers" speech, Lt. Colonel Oliver North presented his lame defense of illegal activities, "I was only following orders," with "the same quaver of voice and modicum of manly moisture in the eye that had served Nixon so well."

John Wayne, the consummate movie hero, spoke for his generation when he advised that he might cry for his horse, for his dog, or for a friend, but never for a woman. Since a man is supposed to be the boss, it is his job to hold back tears so the women and children can cry. Male competence has traditionally been defined in the mold of the fictional cowboy—and fictional indeed, considering John Wayne did whatever he could to avoid fighting any real wars. Nevertheless, his stoicism, restraint, and inexpressiveness, except with a fist or gun, has become the model for strength in men. Feelings, and tears, get in the way.

Forgetting How to Cry

As the men testified earlier, it is not uncommon for young boys to have their tears humiliated or even beaten out of them. This is a ritual trauma repeated again and again by coaches, fathers, siblings, or friends:

> I used to be a crybaby. I once got my whole little league team to cry, I was so good at it. I just used to hate to lose. I was on a team that was terrible. We were in the minors. Unlike the teams in the majors that got full uniforms, we only had T-shirts and caps. We couldn't even win a game, and I would cry every time. This one particular time on my birthday I was crying especially hard and then other guys started crying as well. Our coach went nuts! He called me the biggest crybaby of all.

I went through a long period of stifling my tears after that. I felt numb whenever I wanted to cry. I can now recite a long list of times I *didn't* cry—at Kennedy's assassination, the breakups with girlfriends, deaths, births. . . . All I ever felt and could express was anger. I'm sure people liked me a lot better when I was a crybaby.

Another story of a man who has forgotten how to cry is described in Gus Lee's novel *Honor and Duty*. The hero is a young cadet at West Point. He is a man's man, a fierce warrior and disciplined soldier who has not cried since he was nine. He teases his sister for crying, begs her to stop, feeling so uncomfortable he gets up to leave. He fights his own tears, wills himself to maintain the control befitting a soldier:

> I lurched up and stumbled to the bathroom on feet that were not mine. The pressure behind my eyes, in my head, swelled against the walls. . . . Muscles convulsing, I groaned, crushed my mouth with my right hand, knocking my glasses off onto the hard floor of the lavatory as the tears rushed out and noises that were foreign to me escaped from my throat and ears. I began hitting the walls until I was weak and wet. . . ."

Yet, far from release, the young cadet feels immoral and weak having cried. His sister, aghast at the intensity of his display, asks him what is wrong, then realizes he doesn't know how to cry. He is speaking a foreign language.

In another example from fiction describing how a man had forgotten how to cry, Pat Conroy's character in *Beach Music* muses about what he has lost:

> I stood before my unconscious mother without allowing myself to feel a thing. My own tears seemed landlocked and

frozen in a glacier I could not reach or touch within me. What kind of a man was I who could not even bring himself to weep at the bedside of his dying mother?

The kind of man, Conroy writes, who was raised in a small town to be the consummate Southern gentleman—stoical, hard, emotionally restricted, and without ever a tear in sight. Interesting that such poetic descriptions of men's experiences with crying (or lack thereof) are only found in fiction—where it is safe to discuss such feelings under the guise of imagination.

LEARNING TO CRY AGAIN

The impact of feminism, the men's movement, gender equality, and values of androgyny will make it easier for men to weep more openly. This is especially the case when men express tears that originate in the distinctly male ways in which they relate to others as fathers and sons, brothers and lovers, friends and warriors.

When a man's man like retired General Norman Schwarzkopf can cry patriotic tears so openly, it makes it easier for the rest of us. In his own statement about what tears mean to him, the general explains: "I don't think I would like a man who is incapable of enough emotion to get tears in his eyes."

Men are learning to cry again by taking their cues from women. Unfortunately, the reverse is true as well—women are learning from men that it is unseemly and unproductive to shed tears if you want to succeed in this world. These same style differences are reflected not only in emotional

expressiveness but in the whole way that each gender approaches challenges.

Women are trying to teach men to cry just as men are
influencing women to stop crying, to ignore their emotions
in favor of thinking, to minimize the process in the search for
goals. As one man succinctly puts it:

> I know my wife is trying to reach out to me. She's trying to
> tell me something, but for the life of me, I can't hear her. When
> the tears fall, I just walk away.

In the face of tears, men become logical. They offer plat-
itudes ("Now, now. It will be okay.") that demonstrate clearly
they don't really understand. Men want to fix what they see
is a problem: "How do I turn the damn spigot off?"

When a man cries, it signals deep, core feelings. If a
woman responds to his tears in the same ways in which she
would prefer to be responded to in similar circumstances, a
misunderstanding is likely. One man explains: "I wish my wife
would not make a big deal out of it. I already feel embarrassed.
Just leave me alone and let me work it out."

Of course, these gender generalizations only contribute
to continued myths that all men or all women act in a particular way. There are as many exceptions to the rule—men who
wish to be comforted when they cry, women who prefer to
weep in solitude. Likewise, there are many men who have in-
finite patience and sensitivity when responding to tears, and
many women who cannot stand being in the same room with
someone who is crying. Perhaps the biggest misconceptions
of all continue to persist because people simply don't talk
about their tears to others very often. There are legions of

women walking around who harbor the secret that they don't cry much at all, yet to admit such a thing implies that somehow they are defective. This is exactly the case with men who are private, fluent criers; they guard their secret for fear of being judged as weak and spineless.

Exceptions to the Rule

We often speak of men and women as if their behavior is easily predicted by their gender, yet the differences among members of the same sex are as great as those between the genders. In general, it is true that women cry more than men. However, it is also the case that some men cry quite a lot and some women never shed a tear. The problem doesn't seem to be in the frequency with which a person cries, but in what he or she thinks crying means.

In learning to cry again, some men have taken it upon themselves to risk rejection and disapproval by reclaiming their tears. They have discovered that by allowing themselves to express feeling more authentically, they are being more honest and sincere, more true to their inner nature that had long ago been conditioned to cut off the possibility of tears. They are learning about the benefits of such vivid, essential experience—the powerful release, the experience of being so alive in the moment, the intimacy that can be created with others who can handle the emotional intensity.

Men are also learning about the price that is paid for expressing their tears. Prior to beginning the process of writing this book, I was pretty much like most men I know. I liked to think of myself as fairly sensitive; actually, I was darn sure that I could express my feelings as well as anyone. Why then, I mused, had I not cried in years? I could actually count the number of times I cried in all my adult years.

I became uncomfortable with the realization that perhaps I wasn't as emotionally fluent as I believed. After all, I reasoned, a man who won't let himself cry never lets himself get to the point where he feels very much at all.

In a series of incidents that will be described in the next chapter, my ability and willingness to cry in response to a whole assortment of situations had me feeling a bit giddy. A whole new world of possibilities was opening up to me, one that left me feeling confused, drained, and altogether uncertain whether I liked this new language. Whereas some of the people in my life embraced the new, more emotionally expressive man, and others didn't seem to notice or care one way or the other, quite a number of people began to feel very uneasy whenever I cried, or even tried to talk about experiences that had moved me to tears. I learned a lesson that many women have known for a long time: it is not enough to be able to cry fluently; you must also know how to do so discretely.

There is a whole movement afoot. More and more men are teaching themselves to cry again, experimenting in much the same, halting way that they once learned to walk and talk. They are testing the water a bit, shedding a tear here and there, and then watching carefully to see how they feel afterward, and how others react. If they are satisfied with the result, they let themselves go a little more at a time.

For other men, the evolution of their tears proceeds with the same sporadic, serendipitous progress that is part of the way behavior develops for any species. One day, a man is minding his own business, taking care of the usual routines of his life, and some dramatic incident occurs. It may be a tragedy like the death or rejection of a loved one. It could be a major disappointment involving financial or career problems. It could result from a reminiscence with his mother on the phone, or watching his child sleeping in her bed. It could even involve a transcendent experience that was ignited by a moving experience with Nature or God. In whatever its form, this experience was so significant that the man's usual reserve was overridden by a surge of emotional power that could not be restrained. Tears appeared of their own accord, against all efforts of protest.

The result of this unplanned and unanticipated crying response is that many men discover that they quite like the freedom of expressing their pain and joy in more full and complete ways. They have made exceptions to their rule of staying in control. Following the laws of learning theory, when a result becomes satisfying it tends to be repeated. Men who have not cried much at all and then finally give in to the impulse against their will, learn that they like the feeling of letting themselves go—if they are honored and respected for their emotional transparency. But with the mixed messages that men receive, this reaction is by no means assured.

Mixed Messages

For many centuries men have been taught to feel proud of their emotional restriction. Now the rules are changing in such a way that men who can't or don't cry risk being accused of insensitivity. Yet there are dangerous mixed messages to consider: if a man cries openly, he also may be seen in the same light as women—who are often judged as emotionally unstable.

Men are just as handicapped by the prohibitions they feel against being able to reveal themselves authentically and openly as women feel they are at a disadvantage by their emotional transparency. Men would like to cry more and women wish to cry less.

I make this statement more as a metaphor than as an actual reflection of reality, although this observation is certainly true for many people. Men could learn from women how, by releasing their tears, they could become more open and genuine without feeling apologetic. Likewise, women could learn from men how to be more proactive in their struggle to have their ways of knowing and expressing themselves validated.

The language of tears has many dialects, some of which are regionally based, others are certainly influenced by biological factors. Yet, just as a nation can only survive if it can find a common tongue for all its people while still tolerating individual and group differences, so too must we find a universal form of emotional expression. Tears are that language, even if there are different accents and peculiarities in syntax, grammar, and vocabulary.

Crying is what brings us together. Regardless of our gender or culture, tears are understood by all to mean that we are sincerely moved by something within us or within our field of perception. In order for these experiences to have constructive meaning, our tears must be responded to in ways that enhance rather than diminish us.

8

crying and personal transformation

There comes a point in any serious investigation when we wish to move from a level of understanding to one of action. However interesting the previous discussions about the origins, functions, and variations of tearfulness have been, there is also a desire to apply what is known to our own lives and those of our loved ones.

What should be most clear by now is that crying is a healthy and necessary human process that is an integral part of our existence. Whether such tearful episodes add further fuel to the fires of distress, soothe the burns and heal the scars, or release glorious feelings of peace and transcendence depends very much on how we are able to apply our understanding of the phenomenon of crying.

Tears are the most visible symbol of human intensity. They show themselves only during those times when people are most emotionally charged, for better or worse. During such episodes, we are sometimes at a point of surrender. We turn ourselves over to our feelings, helpless to do anything but let pain bleed out of our eyes. Yet this is also a time of opportunity, a period in which dramatic changes are possible—if only we seize the moment in a constructive way.

In this chapter, and the one that follows, you will apply the concepts learned previously in the book to process your own tearful experiences, as well as those of others around you. Before we move on to a discussion of the best ways to deal with other people's tears, let's first consider what you can do to make the most of your own crying experiences, to listen to your language of tears, and to transform yourself as a result of what you learn from your most articulate inner voice.

TEARS AND CONSTRUCTIVE CHANGE

Emotional crises lead to constructive transitions only when tears are worked through in such a way that they become symbols of triumph rather than of defeat. Crying experiences are critical incidents in our lives; they can take us deeper into despair, or with concerted effort lead us to new levels of personal transformation. Based largely on the research of Laura Rice, Leslie Greenberg, and Jeremy Safran, as well as my own work, I can offer the following method by which tears can be worked through to the point of resolution. While this process is often completed in the context of a helping relationship, such as between a therapist and client, by now you are equipped with sufficient background about this subject to initiate many changes on your own.

I begin with a story of my own, one that we will follow through each successive stage in this process of personal transformation that is sparked by tears. What allowed these changes to take place for me, just as it would for you, was the willingness to explore the language of my tears, to acknowledge their legitimacy and attend to their underlying meaning.

Acknowledging the Tears

I had cried a few times as an adult, but not very often. Even during those rare times, it would take a lot for me to admit that tears were actually present. I became an expert at the casual arm wipe, removing any evidence that might betray my inner feelings. I was quite proud, actually, that any negative feelings were not really part of my life. I was a master of self-control.

A single incident changed this lifelong pattern. While the adventure itself was life-threatening and therefore memorable, it was my intensely tearful reactions to what happened to me that actually sparked a number of changes I have made since these events. My life changed for the better not because of what happened to me but because of the uncharacteristic way that I acknowledged my tears.

I had been out hiking by myself for several days in an isolated wilderness area in New Zealand. After six hours walking along a rugged coastline, I came to a bay that I had to cross in order to reach the camp where I would be spending the night. I had been told by park rangers that although it was high tide, there would be no problem crossing the inlet—the water would only come up to my waist.

It was getting dark. I could barely see the hut where I was to spend the night just on the other side of the tidal pool. I stripped off my clothes and boots, hoisted the pack upon my shoulders and waded in. The water, though as cold as you might expect for a winter day, became quite manageable. It seemed this would be but a minor inconvenience. In fact, I could feel tears come to my eyes as I scanned the horizon. Here I stood in one of the most beautiful spots on the world.

Lush greenery draped the cliffs. Dense bush, bursting with palms and ferns, surrounded the inlet. The setting sun lit up the sky in hues of orange and pink, reflecting off the water, rippling into the bay, surrounding me with color.

The water got deeper, crawling up my thighs with each step, first to my waist, then to my chest. Twenty minutes had gone by while I had been admiring the scenery during this leisurely stroll, yet the other side seemed to be drawing further away. I hoisted the pack higher on my shoulders and drudged onward. I wondered if maybe when the ranger told me the water was waist deep, he calculated on the basis of someone taller than me. I thought of turning back, but that would mean spending the night outside in the woods. I was already wet and cold so there seemed no choice but to continue forward.

The water rose higher and higher on my body, inching up my chest to my neck, then my chin. At this point I had the heavy pack balanced on my head. My neck and shoulders ached from the strain. My feet were becoming bruised and scraped from the rocks and shells that lined the bottom. Panic started to well up in my throat, and tears began to trickle down my cheeks, adding to the ocean of seawater. I refused to acknowledge my crying, any more than I would admit how afraid I really was.

It was at this point that I noticed how badly I was shivering. I turned to see how far I had come—about halfway, I calculated optimistically. I can do this, I thought. There is no other choice. I redoubled my efforts, shuffling along on my tiptoes, trying to keep my head and pack above the water. I could feel my energy draining away, the cold seeping into my bones. Just at the point I thought of dumping the pack and swimming for the shore, I noticed the water level going down a little. When a few steps later the water level returned to my chin, I stifled a sob building up in my throat.

I had seen movies where the hero was in such a situation as this but he always appeared stoic in his emotional restraint. I imagined John Wayne or Indiana Jones or Davy Crockett in a fix like this. They would *never* cry. Hell, they'd be laughing right about now, enjoying this little dip. Why am I such a wimp, I scolded myself, shamed in what I saw as weakness.

The beautiful sunset was now gone. The light was grey and dull as night descended. I tiptoed along the bottom, numb and resolute, aiming for the beach that finally seemed within reach. There were tears no longer. In fact, I couldn't feel a thing.

I now knew that something was terribly wrong. I was shivering uncontrollably. My thinking seemed confused. I couldn't make my hands work, to put my clothes back on or tie my boots. My legs were rubbery and my feet were raw from walking on the open shells. The wind was picking up, blowing right through me. All I could think to do was run back and forth. I remembered from a Jack London story, the one about building a fire, that the guy stayed alive by running for a while. Then I remembered that he died anyway, and for the first time I felt the terror of my predicament.

I felt no pain or discomfort any longer, as if I was detached from my body. My brain, however, reminded me of its own anguish. I saw flashes of my wife and son. I imagined how they would react when I didn't return. I had no right to subject them to the aftermath of my carelessness. I pictured my son reacting to the news, growing up without a father. I felt so, so sad. I began crying anew, no longer for myself but for those I love.

Then I realized all at once that I had hypothermia. "So this is what it feels like," I whispered out loud. My mind felt like mush, as unstable as my legs. I knew that I would die unless I could get warm fast. I was now panicking, so I started running through weeds and bush towards a light I saw glinting through the trees. I heard voices.

I cried for help. Please help me. The people on the porch of the tramper's hut were stunned as they saw me stumble out of the night, dripping wet, disoriented, in shock. I wondered why they were just staring at me, until I realized that my cries for help never left my brain. My last conscious thought, as I fell into one man's arms, was how silly I must look half-naked with a pack on my back.

Later, with an audience eager to hear my story, I appeared remarkably composed. No big deal, I told them. Just a close call that was averted by the quick action of my new friends. That night, while everyone else slept peacefully, I lay in a pool of tears. I could not stop thinking about how close I had come to leaving my family in their own eternal pain. I kept seeing my son's face, hearing him ask his mother what happened and why. The shivers returned in waves throughout the night, as if the seawater had penetrated every pore and needed to empty out through my eyes. It was as if years of restraint that I had carefully maintained now melted away.

I had cried several times during the previous hours, each time for a different reason. I had shed tears of joy and elation, of fear and apprehension, of frustration and subsequent determination. I had cried to express anger, but also relief. My tears communicated the sadness I felt, as well as gratitude toward my saviors. Yet all these very different emotional reactions were united not only in the seawater that enveloped my body but in the tiny drops that ran from my eyes.

It was in the act of acknowledging my tears that an adventure began for me that was far different from the one that had just ended at the inlet. By listening to my tears and uncovering their hidden meanings I was able to initiate a number of changes in my life, in both the ways that I thought about myself and the means by which I expressed my feelings to others.

Giving Yourself Permission

As should be clear from this narrative, what made this tearful experience instructive were two conditions that were met, both unusual for me. First, for the first time in a long time I was willing to acknowledge my tears instead of wiping them away furtively. Second, for a change I gave myself permission to cry instead of quickly cutting the tears off.

So preoccupied with other matters of survival, all my usual self-restraint evaporated. Whereas my usual style would have been to take a few deep breaths, to distract myself with other thoughts, to repeat the usual admonishments of self-control, this time I just let the tears go. Whether through fatigue, overwhelming emotions that could not be restrained, or some inner wisdom that was finally expressing itself, personal growth became possible only because I gave myself permission to cry.

When the circumstances are appropriate, telling yourself

that it is all right to cry is a big deal. What this means, specifically, is that it is safe to cry; the consequences of doing so will not result in critical judgment by others, nor will crying incapacitate you to the point where you can't take care of yourself. Unless these first two conditions are met—that you are willing to acknowledge the fact that you are crying, and that you give yourself permission to continue the process—then all possibility to work through the meaning of this experience abruptly ends.

Staying With the Feelings

Pay attention. When you are crying, be sure to pay *very* close attention to what is going on within you. Crying episodes are altered states of consciousness, not unlike drug states or other times when your perceptions are hypersensitive.

Rather than cutting yourself off from your feelings, immerse yourself even deeper into what you are experiencing. Notice what your body is doing—the shivers and shakes, the sensations in your chest and neck, throughout every part of you. Listen to the sounds you make. Feel, really *feel,* the tears forming in your eyes as they spill over and trickle down your face. Most important of all, attend to the feelings and thoughts within you. At this point, don't try to analyze or make sense of what is happening—just stay with the feelings rather than cutting them off. This will result, naturally, in even greater tear flow.

Whereas initially I had denied the extent of my terror, once I stayed with those feelings, accepted them as a part of me, it was like a wave of intensity came over me. I didn't know that I was even capable of feeling anything so powerfully. I never felt more alive—or frightened. There were times during that long night when I had an option to leave the cocoon of tears, to distract myself with other thoughts, to make myself sleep, but if I had done so I would have lost the opportunity to connect this experience to others in my life.

Making Connections

There comes a point where staying with the feelings is no longer productive; you can stay mired in the muck endlessly, feeling sorry for yourself, helpless to do anything else but re-main immobilized. Tears by themselves are hardly helpful un-less you are willing to balance the intensity of emotion with the other side of your brain that asks some challenging ques-tions: What does this particular incident remind you of? How is it connected to other things you have experienced before?

Tearful events rarely occur in isolation. We each bring a rich history from the past to every new experience in the present. The flashbacks I was having about my boyhood heroes who never cried reminded me of admonishments I had heard throughout my life: to cry, or to let myself feel intensely, would destroy me. I had trained myself with single-minded determi-nation that it was my powers of logic and reasoning that would dominate my being; tears were the enemy, along with all they represented. I thought of my mother, chronically de-pressed throughout most of her life, and how crying had be-come her major form of occupation; tears had been her most frequent companions.

These tears changed my mind. Their role was no less

significant than helping me to redefine what it means to be alive. Once upon a time, as a young man in college, I had resolved that I would never again let anyone hurt me in the way I felt rejected by a woman I had loved. I vowed I would not cry that deeply for anyone, or myself, again. I had decided that such intensity of feeling was greatly overrated. True to my word, for the next twenty-five years I held myself back in all my relationships, in all my emotional reactions to things I experienced. Furthermore, I was *proud* of this masterful control. I bragged to myself, if not to others, that nothing could hurt me ever again. I felt like Superman. However, one small price I paid was the modulation of my feelings.

After my transformative crying experience, I began to change my mind about the advantages of emotional restraint. After all, no longer was I as vulnerable and needy and unstable as I once felt in my youth. In fact, I was a profoundly different person—even though I was still living by the same rules I had formed a long time ago. I made the connection to this obsolete strategy to protect myself that was no longer needed; if anything, it was getting in my way of experiencing greater intensity and intimacy.

Each of these connections to the past only helps you to broaden the context for working through tears. What makes this an opportunity for significant personal growth is the willingness, and ability, to look at the meaning of your experience not in isolation but as part of a bigger picture that includes all the relevant variables. It would have been easy, for example, to write off this whole episode as just a little scare in which the tears meant nothing other than temporary insanity. The fact that this incident did change the ways I live my life is a direct result of being able to draw together a number of different themes that were important.

Decoding the Meanings

As you have noted throughout our previous discussions, tears have many meanings, both on the surface and of symbolic significance. Decoding your own language of tears involves asking yourself what the various parts of you are trying to express. What are you being informed about? What are you saying to others that you are unable or unwilling to say with words? How are your tears trying to be helpful?

What got my attention in a big way was how rare it was in my life for me to let myself get to the point where I risked being out of control to the point of tears. With the prospect of dying, I had considered the ways I had muted my feelings in my relationships. My tears had been saying to me that the self-control I had once so cherished had now become self-defeating. If I was courageous enough to venture out into the wilderness alone, why was I so fearful of facing the deeper parts of me and my relationships with others?

Now, was that what they were *actually* saying? Of course not! Or who cares? That is the initial meaning I created from the experience, a conclusion that would be considerably expanded as I gave the matter more reflection. Over the course of the next several months, I continued to think about the meaning this experience had in my life. More significantly, I continued to cry at a rate that was alarming compared to what I had been used to. It was in the act of talking to others, however, that I was truly able to deepen the effects of what my tears had been communicating.

Reaching Out to Others

Although crying is a distinctly private experience, we have seen how as a language it is a public form of self-expression. Tears are messengers, indirectly linking your nervous system to those of others. While crying is a start in terms of getting feelings out in the open, tears must also be translated into verbal language.

It is through dialogue with others that a kind of transcendent empathy is possible. If your tears help you to appreciate the depth of your feeling, then completing the transformative work involves reaching out to others in a spirit of openness and love. Whereas in the next chapter, we deal more specifically with your role on the other side of tears—that is, when you are responding to someone else—here you are responsible for taking the risk of encountering others on the most basic level of engagement.

When you speak to others you trust about your language of tears, you risk a degree of vulnerability, but also of greater intimacy. It was not enough for me to think about how much I loved my family and friends, how much I take them for granted; I made a commitment to tell people more often how I felt.

The positive effects of a crying experience can be deepened when you test out the new insights in a number of ways. This involves internal experiments in which you play with the idea of redefining yourself in other ways. It also involves testing new ideas during interactions with others.

I felt exhilarated with the realization that I could deepen the intensity of my feelings, and my relationships, if I would learn to reclaim my tears. I began to play with the possibilities, pushing myself, even forcing myself, to squeeze out a few tears during times when ordinarily I wouldn't consider such an unseemly display. Like riding a bike, I discovered that you never forget how to cry even if you have not done it in a while.

Perhaps even more powerful as a means to deepen the effects, I began to talk to others about my experience. I feared that I would be judged harshly, or that people would tell me I was stupid for jeopardizing my life. I also didn't want others to know that someone like myself, who is supposed to be so sensitive, really kept a lid on what I allowed myself to feel.

As it turned out, this was a real turning point during this whole period of transition. What you too are likely to discover is that when you talk to people about your tearful episodes, you will hear other stories in return. And when other people tell you about what they have experienced, you begin to develop another context for what you are reflecting on. You are able to ask yourself not only how a particular incident fits into your previous history but also how it fits in with what others know.

The significance of the tears changes as you reframe the experience in light of other interpretations. Each time I told my story, a person offered another explanation of what had transpired. I was fascinated by all the possibilities, and as I heard more and more perceptions, the story itself began to change—not the narrative details themselves, but the emphasis on different aspects that I hadn't considered important at first telling.

COMPLETING THE WORK

Insight is a wonderful thing, but only if it motivates you to take action. Time and time again, people claim they have reached some new understanding of themselves or the world around them, but that realization never seems to filter down into making changes in behavior. How lovely that you realize that intimacy has been compromised in your life because of too many, or too few, tears. If this insight does not lead you to do anything different in the ways you relate to others, it is inert knowledge without enduring value.

It would not have been nearly enough for me to realize what had been missing in my life and leave it at that. Nor would it have been sufficient to tell the story, focusing on the potential loss of my life rather than the potential gain of my tears. By talking to other people about this experience, especially those who know me well, I was committing myself to act differently. I was warning people to expect a new, more tearful me. I found that I quite liked myself in this new light; I resolved that I would continue to cry as the spirit moved me.

Personal transformation is not only about thinking and feeling differently but also about behaving in new ways. If you have made the appropriate connections, deepened the effects of what you lived through, and created meaning that fits for you, the next step would be to complete the work by initiating changes in the ways you act. Often this involves dealing with unfinished business, feeling greater self-acceptance, and committing yourself to respond in more constructive ways to those around you.

It may help in this process to consult a specialist. No, not an expert on tears—you know more about that now than most professionals. What I am referring to are the limits of what is possible in promoting your own personal transformation without help. In the vast majority of cases, crying represents an opportunity to look at your own behavior and do something about those aspects that are in need of change. As a chronic condition, however, when tears become everpresent and symptomatic of emotional disorder, they are not going to go away without some outside help.

How do you know if you need help or not? Well, one obvious rule of thumb is that if you have exhausted your own resources and the resources of those around you without reducing your distress to manageable levels, it is time to look elsewhere. The professions that practice psychotherapy spend the vast majority of their efforts dealing with chronic depression in which tears play a major part.

Although everyone seems to be jumping on the bandwagon of medicating themselves with Prozac and other antidepressant medications that are supposed to fix chemical imbalances, there are times when chronic tears do result from biologically based disorders. In other instances, a course of therapy can help people to work their way through the various stages described here, which do follow a generic model practiced by many clinicians.

Fluency in the language of tears involves more than just being able to understand and speak to yourself; of equal importance is being able to hear, translate, and talk to others who are tearful. In the next chapter, we look more closely at what therapists and other helpers do to respond to people who are crying.

9

responding to tears

In this chapter we will explore the strategies and skills involved in responding to people in the throes of painful tears. These approaches are derived from our previous discussions, as well as from what experts who respond to tears for a living are inclined to do with those who are suffering.

MAKING A DIFFERENCE

You don't have to be a professional therapist to experience the thrill, even the spiritual transcendence, that comes from helping someone work through tears. There are few other times when you feel more useful.

It is interesting to speculate why we have been programmed in such a way that we're willing to extend ourselves to people with no apparent hope of reward. It would make sense that we would do everything in our power to help our own descendants—but why invest time and energy to aid those who don't share our genes? From an evolutionary point of view, altruism hardly makes sense; there seems to be no biological payoff.

Animals on lookout will send distress signals to their

brethren, even sacrificing themselves to predators in the process. Humans, however, are the only creatures that *choose* to help. We are the only ones with the capacity to respond to others' tears without the prospect of receiving any reward. In his book on compassion in human behavior, Morton Hunt considers this quality as what makes us most special—the willingness to extend ourselves to others in need even though it may not be in our own best interest.

Certainly we choose to help others when we feel like it, but there is also some evidence that distress signals like tears bypass conscious intent, igniting something primal in our nervous system. Yes, tears often make us uncomfortable to be around, but there is also something awfully seductive in them that pulls us in whether we like it or not.

Look closer and you can see some reason why altruism would be rewarded in some way, perhaps through what we sometimes know as the *helper's high,* that transcendent feeling of perfect peace when you know you have made a positive difference in someone's life. There is indeed evidence for a glow of goodwill that is elicited during times that we offer assistance to others, even when our efforts are not necessarily successful. There are actually measurable changes that take place in the body, producing euphoric states.

During those times when you have reached out to someone in pain, especially when it is not part of your job to do so, it feels like your whole life has been redeemed. It is as if by the single act of giving comfort to a lost boy on a street corner, or the cashier who looks low and is perked up by a caring smile, you are saving yourself as well. People speak of feeling tearfully spiritual in a synagogue or church, or watching a sunset on the beach, but for many people the ultimate in spiritual transcendence is reaching out to someone in tears.

You can feel that helper's high hit like a drug. You feel euphoric and giddy. You want to sing or dance or do something with the excess energy coursing through your veins. You have made a difference to someone. Is it God who is rewarding you for this good deed by a solid jolt of goodwill? Or is it a million years of genetic programming that reinforces you for a small gesture that is good for your species? No matter, the effect is the same.

Think about a time when you have offered comfort to someone in tears. Consider the range of feelings you experienced—perhaps helplessness and frustration in the beginning, eventually changing to pride or elation. There are few things as redeeming on this planet than the feeling that through your small efforts you have made a difference.

Reaching Out to Someone Else, or Reaching In to Help Yourself
There are two ways to respond to tears: the first designed to be helpful to the crier, the second to meet your own needs. If we examine those situations in which babies begin howling, we find that parents will either respond in a way that attempts to address whatever they perceive the baby is asking for (food, diaper, comfort, and so on), or they may pacify the infant with a sucking device that plugs the screaming hole.

The ways you react to tearfulness in adults are similar, either driven by an altruistic motive to make someone feel better, or to meet your own needs. Sometimes it is difficult to tell the difference. In a therapy group, the person sitting next to me is telling the story of feeling caught in the middle between her present husband, who wants her to set firmer limits with her son, and her ex-spouse, who is waging a quite different campaign. I see tears forming puddles in her lower lids as she speaks, finally overflowing down her cheeks.

Her makeup is starting to run and she is trying to smudge the tears before they get too far. She is feeling self-conscious and inhibited. I quickly signal for tissue, which I hand to her as I simultaneously put a reassuring hand on her arm. I did this primarily for her. I want to give her permission to cry, to express the frustration and anger she is feeling that she has barely acknowledged. With the comfort of a full box of tissue and my hand resting on her arm, she continues to talk through her tears in the direction of some sort of resolution.

A few minutes later in her soliloquy she has reached an impasse. If she does what her husband wants, she feels like she is betraying her son. If she gives in to her son, she will anger her husband and accede to the wishes of her ex-husband. No matter what she decides, she feel helpless. *So do I.* This time I reach down for tissue to stop her tears but I am doing it for me, not her. As I hand her the "pacifier," I am signalling her this time to dry the tears. I am tired of them. They are making me feel impotent. Sure enough, the gesture works and she regains composure. She also stops working on the issue on a primary, emotional level and instead begins intellectualizing and analyzing the proceedings. I am now feeling much better.

There is thus a basic question to ask yourself when you respond to someone in tears: Are you doing this to be helpful to her or to help yourself? Often both motives are at work. Although you might be primarily altruistic in your intent, there is a personal payoff as well.

One good rule of thumb is to ask yourself whom you are really helping by your gesture. If you can truly justify that you're not intervening to quiet the noise or to appease your own issues of helplessness, then your effort is more likely to be helpful. If, however, you are really meeting your own needs, accept the reality that you may be doing more harm than good.

When I offered a tissue to silence the tears in the second instance, I was meeting my own needs to feel useful. I cut off the work she was doing, perhaps even needed to complete, and also prevented myself from looking at my own painful issues. Only later did I realize how familiar this interaction felt to the relationship I had with my depressed mother when as a little boy I tried so hard to stop her from crying.

When People Block Their Ears to Tears

Most people experience a state of empathic distress when in the company of someone who is crying. In the deeper recesses of your brain, this pain signal activates arousal in you, providing a state of discomfort that can be reduced only one of three ways: by helping the person in need, by leaving the vicinity as quickly as possible, or by rationalizing that you really cannot do much to be of assistance. Of course, there is an alarming amount of historical evidence to indicate widespread use of the latter two coping strategies.

For those who protest that the holocausts of the Crusades, Nazi Germany, or Bosnia could never happen again, there is considerable evidence to the contrary. There have been some disturbing investigations of bystander apathy during times when a person is in great need of help. The case of Kitty Genovese in New York City back in 1967 is one such example that raised a number of difficult questions. Here was a woman who was murdered brutally, stabbed dozens of times over a period of an hour, while thirty-eight witnesses watched from their windows without doing anything to help, even to call the police.

Psychologists have replicated circumstances in which people are crying for help, only to find that others ignore the distress and walk away. When responsibility for care can be spread around a crowd, individuals are less likely to offer assistance than if they were alone. There is thus a social ethic to ignore tears if there are others around who could be helpful, a marked reluctance to feel commitment and responsibility toward taking care of others who are obviously in need.

If you can't ignore the problem, the next most favored method to reduce discomfort in the face of distress calls is to justify your inaction: "It's not my problem." "Someone else is better equipped than I am to deal with this situation." "I'd probably only make things worse."

When there is a fear of looking bad—to others who might judge you, or to your own conscience—then there is greater dissonance created by not acting. It is perhaps optimistic if not naive to hope that more people will feel a greater responsibility for taking care of others. There is no human skill more critical than the means by which to respond effectively to people who are tearful.

The act of helping takes us out of ourselves. The simple gesture of asking someone how you can be helpful—or even better, sensing just what is needed and offering it without hesitation—is among the most valuable things you can ever do.

If crying is one of the single most basic human reflexes, then responding to tears is another.

STRATEGIES FOR RESPONDING TO TEARS

Everyone is an amateur at offering comfort to others during tearful times. We have some experience trying to be helpful, sometimes feeling quite successful, other times feeling fairly useless. In spite of our natural tendency to reach out to others, and in spite of our skills acquired along the way, there is so much more to learn about how to respond best to people who are crying. In the section that follows, we review some of the basic and advanced methods that are most useful in making a positive difference to those most in need of help.

When to Talk, When to Cry

I know I had this constriction settling in my chest. I was working with this wonderful therapist. I had been really working hard not to cry and he gave me permission to let go. At one point he asked me what I was afraid would happen. The image that I had, which I later learned is a fairly common one, is that I would dissolve in a pool of tears.

As soon as I verbalized that, I lost the fear of disintegrating. It was like the explosion of a dam—the tears just poured out. That was a turning point for me. I felt such calmness and peace and relief afterwards.

As is evident from this man's description of his experience, among the most critical decisions to be made when responding to tears is when to encourage someone to let go and just cry, and when to interrupt that person to talk through the experience. Since crying often flows from the feeling of being overwhelmed, the helper's role is often to facilitate the articulation of what the tears are saying. To do so means recognizing when to interrupt the flow and when to allow the tears to continue.

Like the surf of an ocean, crying has stages in which it slowly gathers momentum, builds in power and force, until it dissipates its energy with a crash, then a whimper. For each person, the critical moment of release may occur at a different point—with the vocal wail, an expulsion from the diaphragm, abrupt movement, or the flow of tears themselves. It is at that point that the person is not only ready to talk but needs to do so. Your job is to wait until that critical moment to invite the person to elaborate on the language of tears.

In the detailed analysis of one such crying event, psychologist Susan Labott and colleagues tracked the apparent sequence of events that led to the weeping. After expressing her pain and anger, the client felt heard and understood by her therapist. Offering support and reassurance, the therapist further linked present feelings with past losses. Sobbing began as the client spoke of the neglect that she suffered. When the therapist encouraged her to reexperience the feelings of hurt and anger, there was a peak of emotional arousal.

Once the therapist encouraged her to make sense of what was happening, there was a noticeable settling of affect. The crying may have been for her present predicament, but the intense weeping was for events in the past. The authors point out that it was the safety the client felt in the clinician's presence that permitted her to shed these therapeutic tears.

In order for this process to unfold, the tearful person must feel the invitation to let himself go. This is far more difficult than it sounds, even for professionals. Holly Forester-Miller describes how, as a beginning therapist, she struggled with her own feelings of uneasiness around others' pain:

> I was counseling a twelve-year-old boy named Brian. In our first session, as I was practicing empathy to the hilt, Brian started to cry. Instantly, my heart and mind started racing, and I thought, "Aha! It works! I hit on something." Then, "Oh no! Now what? The poor kid. He looks like he is in so much pain. He must be so uncomfortable and embarrassed. It hurts me to see him in so much pain. How can I make him comfortable? Oh, look at those huge brown eyes; he looks like Bambi did when he found out his mother had died."
>
> Well, I quickly changed the subject. Brian obliged and changed gears with me, drying his tears. Although he brought up the original subject twice more in the session, I managed to side-step it and keep the session on a superficial, cognitive level. In other words, I ran like hell. I knew immediately what I *should* have done, but tears from a twelve-year-old boy caught me off guard and elicited some of my own scary feelings. So, I played it safe. Buy what price did Brian pay for *my* discomfort?

If even therapists have difficulty being with people when they are crying, it's apparent that "civilians" as well have work to do to increase their comfort with tears. This grounded position of feeling clear and receptive is necessary in order to decode what tears are communicating.

Focusing on Recovery

For many years it has been assumed, following Freud's lead, that catharsis of emotion is inherently therapeutic. The simple but moving act of expressing feeling was thought to release pent-up toxic energy in such a way that you would be left free of your burdens. Thus, crying has been held in the highest esteem by members of the counseling profession as the clearest evidence that good work is taking place.

We have our ways to help people release their tears. We make clients relive meaningful experiences, and every time they try to escape, we gently—sometimes forcefully—push them back into the flames. We listen carefully to the nuances of unexpressed feelings that are lurking beneath the surface, and then bring them into the open with a dramatic flourish: "I hear a lot of pain in what you are saying. You are feeling alone and overwhelmed." Tears are the inevitable result.

It is, therefore, disheartening if not embarrassing when we learn that things we have always believed to be therapeutic may not be so helpful after all. Car manufacturers send out recall notices when they discover some defective part or labor. In light of recent research on the subject of emotional catharsis, perhaps therapists should do the same. We should recall all the clients we have ever seen whom we have encouraged to shed tears for their own sake. We now have indications that emotional arousal and expression as an end in itself may not only be useless but may even be harmful. Unless people are helped to complete the arousal cycle to a point of returned deactivation, emotions that have been turned on may continue to spin out of control.

It is only in the act of resolution that crying can become therapeutic. In their analysis of this phenomenon, Jay Efran and Tim Spangler found that it is the *recovery* from tears, not the act of crying itself, that is experienced as most therapeutic. The implications of this are, then, that helping people to feel comfortable crying is indeed important, but not without also helping them to dry their eyes and make sense of the experience.

A Systematic Approach

This process is similar to any therapeutic journey. First, genuine feelings are brought into awareness, not just intellectually but experientially. It is not enough to talk about experiences; one must live them. Next, new meaning is created through systematic inquiry, providing a thorough understanding of the issues involved. These insights hopefully lead one to assume greater responsibility for what one's tears are communicating. Since they are part of you—they flow from your eyes, they emerge from your internal processes—it is within your power to stop them. This task is completed by identifying those feelings that are not very helpful and converting them into others that are more fully functional.

It isn't necessary to get a graduate degree in psychology, social work, or counseling to improve your own ability to be helpful to others. I have spent the last few years working with teachers in various countries to help them to increase their skills at responding to the emotional needs of children. In just a few hours of systematic instruction and practice, it is possible to make a significant difference in the ways in which you can provide help to others.

Here is a brief review of those principles, derived from what therapists do in their professional efforts:

Adopt helping attitudes. One of the most healing aspects of any helping encounter is the feeling that no matter what you say or do, no matter how vulnerable you might be, the other person will still be respectful and accepting. The difference between relating to someone as a friend versus doing so as a helper is that in the latter case we suspend all judgments, stay neutral, and respond empathically. These attitudes are absolutely critical when responding to people who are crying, conveying that even though you may not agree with everything they are doing or saying, you still accept them unconditionally.

Assess what you believe is happening. Do this *with* the other person; nobody likes to be analyzed like some insect under scrutiny. Enter the world of the other person. Try to feel what he is experiencing. Reflect back what you sense, hear, see, feel. Help the person to talk through the tears in a dialogue that might resemble the following:

Him: [*Sits quietly, head down, arms encapsulating himself, gently rocking, tears falling.*] It's just . . . just that [*sobs*] . . . I can't seem . . . can't seem to get control of things any more.

You: It seems difficult for you to even put your thoughts into words right now.

Him: [*Looks up. Smiles briefly. Shakes his head in agreement.*] Yeah, you got *that* right.

You: Yet you *are* being really clear and articulate right now.

Him: [*Looking puzzled*] Huh? I don't know what you mean.

You: Just that you are speaking through your tears. They are speaking to both of us. What do *you* think they are communicating?

And so the dialogue continues, usually quite haltingly, but nevertheless progressing in the direction of defining the moment and its underlying meanings.

Don't give advice. When people are first learning to operate in helpful roles one of the greatest challenges is to avoid telling the other person what to do. Most human difficulties are not so simple that someone else can listen for a few minutes and then tell you exactly what you need to do. When you indulge yourself in such behavior, you are usually not doing so for the benefit of the other person (who almost never follows what she is told) but to assuage your own sense of helplessness. Giving advice only reinforces the idea that the person needs someone like you to tell him what to do. If by some miracle this works out well, you have taught this person to come to you again next time. If things don't work out, then you will be held responsible.

For these reasons, it is best to keep your goals somewhat modest. Your intent is not to change this person, nor even to promote growth. Your role is only as a loving and compassionate listener who is open to hearing what the tears are saying.

Don't try to do too much. Just listen. Carefully. Don't underestimate the power of your full and complete attention. The more you attempt to intrude forcefully, the more likely you will be to do harm as well as good. It is not your role or responsibility to fix things, but rather to provide a supportive relationship so that the other person feels cared for.

It is altogether rare that we ever have the undivided attention of someone else. So often, even with those we love the most, we speak to them as we are engaged in other things—opening mail, looking at the television, listening to the radio, waving to someone else. It feels so wonderful to have someone put all distractions aside, face you fully, and communicate with every part of his or her being that for the next few minutes you are the most important person in the world.

Concentrate on basic helping skills. Concentrate on attending fully to the other person. This means communicating with your eyes, facial expressions, body posture, and verbal responses that you are intensely tracking everything that is being said, through both words and tears. It would be difficult to underestimate the value of basic skills that involve reflecting back what you hear and sense. Through such responses you communicate that you heard what was said. More than that, you *prove* that you understand.

Your primary role, then, is to help the person to talk in an open and free manner. Reflect back what you sense, hear, see, feel. Help the person talk through the tears. Through gentle, open-ended questions, help the person to explore at a deeper level: What is going on for you right now? What would you like to see happen? What are your tears saying?

Try reframing. This advanced strategy applies a simple premise: by changing the way you define your predicament, you can dramatically alter the way you react to what is going on. This method is applied quite frequently by members of the clergy when they reframe the tragic finality of death by saying, "The departed has passed on to a better place. He is resting peacefully now."

Essentially the object of this strategy is to help the person to think differently about what he or she is experiencing. Crying is not a sign of weakness or helplessness but rather evidence of your emotional investment. The result of this reframing is that the person in tears will often feel less helpless.

Gently confront distortions. The key word here is *gently*—people in tears are in no mood to have someone in their face. Often they are not yet ready to be confronted; your attempts must be very diplomatic and tentative so you don't risk making the person feel criticized or judged. For example, if a person said: "It's all so hopeless," you could gently respond with: "You mean it seems that way just now."

It is important to be gentle and diplomatic, but make some tentative efforts to point out discrepancies between the person's exaggerations and reality. Back off if you observe that the person is not ready to hear what you are offering.

If the person feels accepted, heard, understood, validated, and honored while revealing frightening, vulnerable aspects of herself, she will feel safe enough to experiment with alternative ways of being. The mutual sharing of feelings becomes a model for other relationships in the future.

Challenge the self-defeating ways that people think about their tears. We have seen how negative feelings, with their resultant tears, do not emerge out of thin air but represent reactions to particular cognitive activity. In the words of cognitive therapists Albert Ellis, Aaron Beck, or Jeffrey Young, we make ourselves cry based on how we choose to interpret what is happening in the world—whether it is happening *to* us or whether we are perceiving events in a particular way and thereby setting up inevitable emotional consequences. If in response to disappointment you say to yourself things like, "This is awful. I'll *never* get what I want. I don't deserve to be happy," it is highly probable you will end up in tears. If, on the other hand, you react with a more level-headed "This *is* disappointing. Oh well. How can I approach this differently?" you are also likely to feel sad and frustrated, but to a lesser degree.

Separate your stuff from theirs. Therapists call it counter-transference when the helper starts working through personal issues instead of attending to the person allegedly being helped, but I am speaking more generally about those times when your buttons are being pushed by what the other person is experiencing. One of the reasons we find it so difficult to be with people who are crying is that it reminds us of our own sense of helplessness. We want people to show strength because it reassures us of our own inner fortitude. When I am with someone in tears, it often makes me feel hopeless as well. I want to stop that person's tears so I can feel better.

Other signs and symptoms that you may have lost your perspective and are deep into your own issues instead of the issues of those you are trying to help are

- You are finding it difficult to feel empathic and compassionate towards the other person.
- You are finding it difficult to understand what the other person is trying to communicate. Your reflections and interpretations are consistently off the mark.
- You are feeling especially frustrated, blocked, and helpless with the person.
- You are aware of parallel issues of your own that crop up as you listen to the other person.

- You are finding it difficult to concentrate on what the other person is saying because you are so deeply into reflections about your own life.
- You are feeling impatient because the person is not moving along as quickly as you would prefer.
- You are aware that you are working harder than the other person is.

When you are in a helping role, it is extremely important not only to monitor what is happening with the tearful person, but also what is going on within yourself.

Encourage the person to get some help. Recognize the limits of what you can do as an amateur. Even with your intense desire to be helpful, and some extra preparation, you still can't offer the kind of in-depth help that many people need, especially those who are lost in a world of tears for a prolonged period of time. Under such circumstances, the best thing you can do is to urge them to get some help from a professional, whether a therapist, counselor, or member of the clergy.

A professional helper can diagnose the exact nature of the problem, build a relationship that is specifically designed to promote changes, assess for possible medical complications and medications, initiate systemic changes within the family, and guide deep explorations into possible causes. In addition, suicidal potential can be assessed for those who are severely depressed and appropriate steps can be taken to protect the person from harm. Your job in such circumstances is to make sure the person follows through on the decision to seek professional help and to make certain that a good match is found between the person and the particular helper. Too often people give up if they don't hit it off with the first person they contact.

A Simple Hug

The methodology just described relies primarily on verbal interactions with a person in tears. But perhaps the simplest but most powerful means to comfort someone who is crying is the one that we learned first in life.

Among the most thorny problems that pediatricians deal with on a daily basis are the frustrated complaints of parents who can't figure out what to do with their babies who won't stop crying. Pediatric journals are filled with articles that speak about the need for *soothability* in the management of crying infants. This means lowering the arousal level so that the child can regain control. Through soft reassurance, singing, rocking, as well as administering a bottle, nipple, or pacifier, calmness is hopefully restored.

Of course, anyone who has ever been a parent, or taken care of a baby knows there are times when nothing works. I once spent four consecutive hours walking around our neighborhood, two-month-old son in my arms. Every time I stopped moving, his piercing wail would begin again. As long as I stayed in motion, he would remain quiet.

Think about the implications of this clinical management advice designed for infants applied to adults. What is it, truly, that you want from others when you are crying except to be soothed and understood? Often you are crying in the first place because other attempts at communication have proven unsuccessful. As one woman explains:

There is nothing that gets to me quicker than trying to express something to my husband who refuses to hear. I tell him what I want or what I need and he ignores me. If that doesn't work, he tries to tell me that what I want is not really important, or that it isn't possible. Only when I cry does he pay attention to me.

It is at this point that, even though she has her husband's attention, things get worse rather than better: "He gets mad at me. All I want is for him to hold me, to listen to what I'm saying."

In other words, she wants to be soothed—and not by a pacifier but by compassion and caring: "I don't care if he agrees with me as much as I just want him to hear what I'm saying, and to show it by holding me."

This desire to have our language of tears heard and responded to compassionately is so strong that it is one of the major reasons that people seek the services of a therapist. If we do nothing else, we are supposed to be respectful and helpful in the ways we hear and react to tears.

We could also learn a lot from so-called less-developed, agriculturally based communities. In these African, Asian, or South American societies in which mothers carry their babies around for much of the day, there is much less frequent crying. Two physicians, Urs Hunziker and Ronald Barr, sought to simulate this custom by instructing mothers to carry their babies in their arms or carriers for a minimum of three hours a day, in addition to any contact related to feeding or comfort. They discovered that the babies who were part of this group, as compared to a control group that interacted in the normal ways of our culture, cried only half as much as previously. The researchers concluded that perhaps instead of pacifying tears with a bottle, we should be holding babies more.

When we consider the oral indulgences that adults often resort to when feeling stress—cigarettes, alcohol, food, nail biting, drugs—we can easily identify the pattern we learned as infants. Instead of pacifying tears, we should be holding one another more—not only in the physical sense of touching and hugging, but in the larger perspective of offering love and care. Indeed, one of the most effective interventions that can be employed with someone in tears is the simple embrace.

One woman describes the comfort she felt from a simple hug while her husband was dying:

> My husband gave me a safe place to cry. I knew I was okay. Others tried to let me cry alone. Some tried to laugh it off or tease me. They all had different ways of trying to help me deal with my sadness and grief. If it wasn't for my husband, holding me quietly, I don't know how I could have gotten through it all. He allowed those tears to cleanse me.

Know Your Own Limits

There are limits to what you can do with a simple hug, or even a host of therapeutic skills. There are those who are unable to stop crying, or to find meaning in their tears, because their condition is the result of some organic problem. You could be as compassionate and understanding as you like with no visible impact.

Just as there are some people who have never cried emotional tears, there are some folks who can't stop. These *pathological criers* have underlying physical disorders that suppress the part of the brain that controls weeping. They go through life with the uncomfortable condition of being unable to stop the outbreak of tears at inopportune moments, or once tears are flowing, to do anything about it.

There are also cases reported of *unilateral lachrymation*—in which a person cries out of only one eye or the other depending on the situation. In one such instance reported in Australia, a woman somehow was able to control an emotional response that is supposedly an autonomic function. Whenever she thought of her mother, she shed tears out of the right eye; if she thought sad thoughts about her father, the left tear duct activated.

There are people who never cry emotional tears and who cannot remember when it was any different. There have been whole families identified, going back several generations, in which virtually nobody sheds tears. There are also those who are completely out of control in their weeping, and not due to any underlying organic problem. The depth of their depression is such that tearfulness becomes a normal state. They cry themselves to sleep, and their first realization upon waking is that nothing in their lives has changed overnight, sparking another bout of tears.

Probably one of the easiest ways to land yourself in the psychiatric unit of a hospital is to cry too much. Although sometimes this behavior results from voluntary control, often there is some organic problem. In treating excessive crying, it is therefore important to identify what exactly is causing the symptoms.

In one study of hospitalized patients who never stopped crying after surgery, psychiatrist Ronald Green and several colleagues investigated underlying reasons for this behavior. Much to their surprise, only one in five of these patients was suffering from major depression; most of the others had some type of neurological disease, brain disorder, or degenerative condition like multiple sclerosis. They observed distortions in their patterns of crying that distinguished neurologically induced crying from that induced by depression. Most obviously, these patients began weeping suddenly, without provocation or identifiable triggers, as if a switch was turned on and then abruptly turned off.

There is also a condition known as *essential crying,* which involves intense outbursts several times a day. These people are otherwise quite normal and do not show evidence of either medical problems or depression. They report feeling sad during the experience, but it is difficult to determine which causes the other to happen. Are they feeling tearful because they are sad, or are they feeling sad because they are crying? Because there are so few people who have been identified with this condition, we know very little about its origins.

CRYBABIES

The parents of infants and toddlers spend an inordinate amount of time thinking about crying. They want to address their children's needs, yet this signal of upset may also trigger feelings of inadequacy. "If only I was a better parent, my child wouldn't cry like this. I bet other parents would know what to do in this situation."

Magazines like *Parents* and *Ladies Home Journal,* as well as the pediatric journals, are loaded with discussions about how to stop children from crying. Parents wonder: How much crying is too much? Am I doing something wrong? Is my child normal? What can I do to stop the tears?

Tiny Stan Laurels

Usually, the most consistent advice offered is already familiar to you. For infants, crying is the only way that they can talk; it is their language. For toddlers and preschoolers, crying a lot is a sign of emotional sensitivity. In both cases, genetic factors predispose some children (and adults) to be more sensitive than others. Not only do they become tearful more often, but as infants they probably are startled more easily. They tend to laugh more often and react more intensely to anything that is happening. They are also more empathic to the feelings of others.

Extreme emotional sensitivity is both a gift and a curse. While it is true that being teased as a crybaby is not much fun, that showing tears easily communicates vulnerability that is often exploited, this capacity is what allows the same person to be unusually sensitive to others. As babies, such individuals cried not only when they were distressed but whenever they sensed tension or fear in others.

In one article about "tiny Stan Laurels in the schoolyard filled with Oliver Hardys," Lawrence Kutner speaks about how excessive crying can mean something other than an oversensitive disposition. If, for example, there is a sudden change in a child's mood in which the frequency and intensity of tears have significantly increased, you could be looking at a depressive condition that requires treatment.

Other considerations to explore include checking out how the child is being rewarded for tears. People continue to engage in behaviors that work for them. As long as crying brings desired results, whether attention, sympathy, or even frustration on the part of others, it will persist. Once these gains can be identified, intervention takes the form of no longer rewarding that behavior.

Responding to Crying Babies
There are several principles to keep in mind when responding to tearful infants:

- Check off a list of possibilities, one at a time, as to what desire might be communicated by the baby's language of tears: feed me, check my diaper, hold and comfort me, burp me, help me get cool or warm, help me calm down, call my doctor. . . .
- Develop soothing rituals to calm things down both for yourself and the baby. Rocking and singing routines are helpful when they are predictable.
- Carry the baby around with you—that reduces tears by 50 percent.
- Use "shut down" techniques as a distraction. Examples include motion (walking and rocking), visual distraction, sounds (music), sucking (pacifier).
- Use touch liberally, especially patting and massaging.
- Make a list of things you have already tried that don't work. Don't do them any more. Try something else.
- Calm yourself down. The only thing worse than having a baby crying is coping with this situation at the same time that you are feeling out of control. Practice mantras such

as: "This is no reflection on my parenting." "This too shall end." "The baby is just doing the best he/she can." "The baby is not doing this to me."

- Get some support. If you have a partner available, spread the burden of responsibility so that you don't feel so overwhelmed. If this is not feasible, recruit the help of friends, family members, and experienced baby-sitters.

- Explore what you might be doing, or not doing, that is inadvertently increasing the crying frequency. Keep track of the patterns of when the baby cries or not. What has been going on just preceding the outbreak? What might you (or others) be doing unconsciously to reinforce the tears?

Although I am speaking of strategies that are specifically suited for crying babies, the intent of any response to a child or adult is essentially the same. We are all a little afraid of the intensity of emotion that is embedded within the language of tears, yet we are also drawn to reach out to this person. Spiritual writer Thomas Moore speaks of this internal conflict by borrowing from mythology:

> The Greeks told the story of the minotaur, the bull-headed flesh-eating man who lived in the center of the labyrinth. He was a threatening beast, and yet his name was Asterion—Star. I often think of this paradox as I sit with someone with tears in her eyes, searching for some way to deal with a death, a divorce, or a depression. It is a beast, this thing that stirs in the core of her being, but it is also the star of her innermost nature. We have to care for this suffering with extreme reverence so that, in our fear and anger at the beast, we do not overlook the star.

This is indeed one of the greatest challenges in human relationships. During times of tears, we are torn between running to someone in distress, and running away as quickly as we can. We wish to be helpful, yet we also want to protect ourselves from being scalded by the tears. As we become more accepting and comfortable with our own language of tears, we can learn to be more responsive to the needs of others during their times of greatest need.

10

a time for tears

We are approaching a new era in the language of tears, one in which—as never before—the benefits of selective crying are appreciated and the complex nuances of this communication are being understood. In many circumstances, crying has become a statement of courage. It shows a willingness on the part of someone to risk vulnerability by expressing the inner core of felt experience. While it is certainly true that tears are still interpreted as a sign of weakness or instability, more and more we are beginning to accept them as a natural part of human experience.

In this closing chapter, we will review some of our main themes with an eye toward implications for the future—your own as well as what you can expect in our culture at large. Continuing in our role as students of tears, we'll examine the ways that crying is now viewed in the public eye, giving us an indication of where we are headed in the future.

SENSITIVE PUBLIC FIGURES

We hold a fascination for the tears of public figures, whether they are thrust into the spotlight or elected to public office. If the crying frequency of U.S. presidents is any indication of the greater acceptance that people feel toward emotional expression, we seem to be headed in that direction. Whereas a few decades ago, crying in public could destroy a politician's whole career, nowadays this behavior is interpreted differently.

When presidential candidate Edmund Muskie wept in 1972 after a mean-spirited attack on his wife, this was seen as a sign of vulnerability and instability. Could we trust such a wimp to run our country? Although Muskie vehemently denied that he had cried (an even more dramatic commentary on the times), claiming that the wetness on his cheeks was from snowflakes, the damage by perception was done. Crying in public, especially by a man who aspired to control armies, was then universally interpreted as a sign of instability.

In marked contrast, when President Bill Clinton in the 1990s cried in public, his ratings went up. People interpreted his crying as a manifestation of his inner goodness and sensitivity. The same pattern has emerged for other male politicians in the last few decades. President Ronald Reagan made it fashionable to cry patriotic tears, whether mourning the *Challenger* accident or giving tribute to the losses suffered in war. The public loved him all the more. Even President George Bush, who had been fighting his image as wimp, was known to shed a few tears when he had to send soldiers into combat.

We have seen that not only can most contemporary politicians get away with the occasional tears, but a well-timed cry will even enhance public appeal. During a seven-month period, various newspapers documented no fewer than eleven separate instances of tearfulness on the part of Bill Clinton. Most of these cries appeared to be triggered by emotional empathy with victims of disaster—widows of dead soldiers, parents of children who died violently, the plight of the homeless. Clinton's tears, however, have also been triggered by sentimental sources—listening to hymns in church, for example. Yet, in one case it was reported he was even overcome with tears for no apparent reason.

The public seems prepared to accept a tearful president today. We not only tolerate this behavior, we like it! If we believe these tears are genuine and authentic expressions of feeling, rather than manufactured displays for public consumption, then a leader's credibility goes up. This is true not only with respect to politicians but even in the most macho of arenas, professional sports, where crying has become perfectly acceptable.

When Lou Piniella lost the divisional baseball championship game, he cried copiously in front of his teammates. When Jimmy Johnson, former coach of the Dallas Cowboys football team, was faced with his star running back's refusal to sign a contract, he broke out in tears. In fact, some of the best-known and most successful football coaches frequently cry when they are disappointed. Rather than losing respect in the eyes of their players and fans, these emotional outbursts seem to enhance their images as caring guys.

Clearly we are approaching a time for tears.

The Test of Tears

Although we have explored how the rules for a language of tears are different for each gender, culture, era, and family, greater permission to cry has been given to most people. With the notable exception of women in positions of power, tears are increasingly being viewed as a sign of emotional sensitivity rather than instability. The standard of male attractiveness currently places an emphasis on such responsiveness, to both internal turmoil and the plight of others. For women, the rules are far more complex: depending on the situation, context, and audience, tears can either break down barriers or drive others away.

If this is a time for tears, then it is an era of confusion and uncertainty. None of us is quite sure any longer what is expected or what will be tolerated.

There was a time not too long ago when we understood all too well what the consequences of letting our tears flow would be in various circumstances. Now we are not so sure. We can each run through a list in our minds of those with whom it is safe to cry, those with whom we would never do so, and a third group whose reactions would be difficult to predict.

Crying is a dramatic way to find out where you stand in relation to others. It is a test of sorts, the formulation of a critical question: Are you safe enough, accepting enough, for me to reveal my most heartfelt feelings? There are three possible outcomes after letting your tears flow: it will draw people closer to you, it will have no effect whatsoever on your relationships, or it will drive some people away. I contend that the latter group includes exactly the folks you don't want to be around anyway. Isn't it about time you found out where you stand?

I am not advocating tearful outbursts during crucial meetings or conferences with someone in a position of power (although such circumstances often make us want to cry most). Rather, I'm suggesting more fluency in the language of tears. There is no quicker way to find out where you stand with others than to cry in their presence and note how they react. Relationships will often deepen in their level of engagement. We have seen how there are few means of expression that are more effective in building rapport, trust, and closeness.

The risk on your part is to make the language of tears more a part of the ways you express yourself.

Putting Tears to Work

Crying is the language of intimacy. Composed of the same essence that makes up 90 percent of the human body and most of the planet's surface, tears are the stuff of life. They are symptoms of intense feeling and the most visible symbol of what it means to be human. Nothing comes even close in power to the language of tears.

Several points have been emphasized throughout this book. Here, I review each of these themes and predict what they may imply for the future.

- CRYING REPRESENTS THE BEST AND WORST OF WHAT IT MEANS TO BE TRULY ALIVE. Cry too much and you are immobilized; cry too little and you risk being cut off from yourself and others.

Prediction: In statistical terms, there will continue to be regression toward the mean (variations in behavior becoming less pronounced) with regard to intercultural and intergender influences. With mass media bringing generic images into living rooms around the world, social behavior related to crying will become as standardized as English as the common language. Likewise, the historical role specializations between men and women are rapidly breaking down. Just as we'll see more women in traditional male positions of authority (litigators, politicians, executives, heads of household), and more men in comparably traditional positions of nurturance (primary parents, emotional caretakers), so too will we see men acting more like women in their crying and women acting more like men in restraining their tears.

- CRYING OCCURS DURING MOMENTS OF OPPORTUNITY. During intense emotional arousal, the biological and psychological systems are in flux. There is temporary chaos and disorientation, conditions that are ripe for promoting changes in future behavior.

    Prediction: Social behavior continues to outpace biological adaption to the changing environment in such a way that emotional stress will continue to place extraordinary demands on people. As society becomes even more technological, more controlled, more complex, the need for crying as a form of intimate contact will be even greater. The future must become a time for tears; if it doesn't, human beings will have lost their compassion and commitment toward mutual caring.

- THERE IS NO OTHER LANGUAGE MORE COMPELLING AND EXPRESSIVE THAN TEARS. Among all forms of communication, crying has the potential to express the greatest variety of messages with the most captivating effects.

    Prediction: As more and more emphasis is placed on the powers of reason, logic, scientific inquiry, empirical verification, and corporate values of efficiency and productivity, crying has its work cut out for itself to hold its special position of prominence among forms of communication. Unless the trend is reversed in the workplace, where crying is restricted to the privacy of bathrooms, the potential value of this miraculous mode of communication will be limited to only the safest of environments. As women wish to gain greater credibility in the world of men, they will continue to restrict their tears in an effort to prove that they have comparable mental toughness. Ironically, as women are headed in one direction, men are headed in the other: masculinity will continue its more flexible evolution in the direction of affording males greater opportunities to express themselves through tears.

• THERE ARE WIDE VARIATIONS IN PATTERNS OF CRYING DEPENDING ON CULTURAL AND GENDER-BASED CONTEXTS. Data about what is considered normal are virtually useless. There are individuals who cry every day and those who never cry emotional tears, yet they may be extraordinarily well-adjusted in their emotional and interpersonal lives. Crying can therefore signal evidence of underlying pathology or of superior emotional expressiveness. One thing is certain: that tears exist not only as a dramatic language system but also as a means to aid the body and mind in their healing functions. Whether for women or men, Ifugaos of the Philippines, Irish Catholics of Boston, or French Canadians of Quebec, crying is instrumental to help stimulate infant development, regulate adult physiological functioning, and express intensity of feeling.

Prediction: Future scientific studies will confirm that crying in moderation produces a number of health and psychological benefits for people—most notably, that it represents a fluent, spontaneous expression of needs within the body and mind.

- LIKE ANY POWERFUL TOOL, THE LANGUAGE OF TEARS CAN BE USED AUTHENTICALLY TO BUILD BRIDGES OF INTIMACY, OR MANIPULATIVELY TO SERVE YOUR OWN INTEREST. It is precisely because crying works so well that it can so easily be abused.

Prediction: No change here. If anything, as higher resolution television, simulated computer experiences, and other technologies satisfy our voyeuristic urges to experience intense feelings vicariously, the hunger for tears—real or contrived—will continue unabated. Any morning talk show can guarantee strong ratings simply by adding a participant who is willing to cry on cue.

NO TIME TO CRY?

Are we truly ready for a time of tears? Would this be a good thing, having people cry more frequently and openly? I hope by now the resounding answer is: absolutely!

Yet the legacy from our ancestors has been to conduct the daily business of our affairs with a minimum of fuss. Emotional spectacles are bad manners, the sign of someone poorly bred or weak-willed. Strength of character has been traditionally measured by a person's ability to suffer silently: "Look at how brave she is, not a tear in her eyes." "I really admire the way he has handled himself—what amazing control!"

The times, however, are changing. There are now several different ways by which we judge internal fortitude. In certain circumstances, people can be admired as much for their courage in showing their feelings as for hiding them. When you reveal the deepest parts of yourself—feelings of ineptitude, of not being good enough, of feeling like a failure, of crying over spilled milk, as well as your pride, caring, spiritual joy, and relief—most people dearly appreciate these admissions of vulnerability. They feel closer to you and more likely to reciprocate with their own personal disclosures.

When you cry aloud over losses—not in self-pity but in grief and pain—you invite others to join you. When you show your tears of joy and empathy, you draw people closer to you, to share your moving experience.

As a student of tears, your original attraction to this subject may have been an intellectual curiosity about a fascinating human phenomenon. These bits of wisdom are certainly interesting, even enlightening in what they say about your most intimate inner life. The question becomes what are you going to do with what you now understand about yourself and others?

Speaking the language of tears fluently is impressive. Understanding the tearful communications of others is even more admirable. What is really extraordinary, however, is whether you decide to apply what you've learned to transform yourself, and others with whom you are in contact, so that your part of the world becomes a safer place to cry.

for further reading

Acebo, C., & Thoman, E. B. (1992). Crying as social behavior. *Infant Mental Health Journal, 13*(1), 67–82.

Anderson, W. T. (1990). *Reality isn't what it used to be.* San Francisco: HarperCollins.

Askew, S., & Ross, C. (1988). *Boys don't cry: Boys and sexism in education.* Philadelphia: Open University Press.

Baddiel, D. (1993). Dambusters. *Sight and Sound, 9,* 37.

Baier, A. (1992). Appropriate ways of crying over milk we chose to spill. *Ethics, 102,* 357–367.

Balswick, J. (1988). *The inexpressive male.* Lexington, MA: Lexington Books.

Barr, R. G. (1990). The early crying paradox. *Human Nature, 1,* 355–389.

Barr, R. G., Konner, M., Bakeman, R., & Adamson, L. (1991). Crying in !Kung San infants. *Developmental Medicine and Child Neurology, 33,* 601–610.

Barton, R. F. (1946). The religion of the Ifugaos. *American Anthropological Association Memoir, 65,* 172.

Bateson, G., Jackson, P., Haley, J., & Weakland, J. (1956). Toward a theory of schizophrenia. *Behavioral Science, 1*(4), 251–264.

Beck, A. T. (1976). *Cognitive therapy and emotional disorders.* New York: International Universities Press.

Begley, S. (1995, March 27). Gray matters. *Newsweek,* 48–54.

Belenky, M. F., Clinchy, B. M., Goldberger, N. P., & Tarull, J. M. (1986). *Women's ways of knowing: The development of self, voice, and mind.* New York: Basic Books.

Belkin, L. (1993, March 10). After first crying, laughing at cancer. *New York Times,* C-1.

Bindra, D. (1972). Weeping: A problem of many facets. *Bulletin of the British Psychological Society, 25,* 281–284.

Boukydis, C. F. Z. (1985). Perception of infant crying as an interpersonal event. In B. M. Lester & C. F. Z. Boukydis (Eds.), *Infant crying: Theoretical and research perspectives.* New York: Plenum Press.

Breuer, G. (1982). *Sociobiology and the human dimension.* Cambridge, England: Cambridge University Press.

Briggs, J. L. (1984). Cited in Calhous, C., & Solomon, R. C., *What is an emotion?* New York: Oxford University Press.

Brody, L. R. (1993). On understanding gender differences in the expression of emotion. In S. Ablon, D. Brown, E. J. Khantizian, & J. Mack (Eds.), *Human feelings.* Hillsdale, NJ: Analytic Press.

Brophy, B. (1987, March 16). Have a good cry—but not at the office. *U.S. News & World Report,* p. 63.

Buchwald, J. S., & Shipley, C. (1985). A comparative model of infant cry. In B. M. Lester & C. F. Z. Boukydis (Eds.), *Infant crying: Theoretical and research perspectives.* New York: Plenum Press.

Buck, R. (1984). *The communication of emotion.* New York: Guilford Press.

Budiansky, S. (1995, June 5). What animals say to each other. *U.S. News and World Report,* pp. 52–56.

Carmichael, K. (1991). *Ceremony of innocence: Tears, power, and protest.* New York: St. Martin's Press.

Choti, S. E., Marston, A. R., Halston, S. G., & Hart, J. T. (1987). Gender and personality variables in film-induced sadness and crying. *Journal of Social and Clinical Psychology, 5,* 535–544.

Chupack, C. (1994, June). Can you stand to see a grown man cry? *Glamour,* p. 128.

Conroy, P. (1995). *Beach music.* New York: Doubleday.

Cosgrove, S. (1990). Borderlines. *New Statesman and Society, 11,* 32.

Cowley, G. (1994, February 7). The culture of Prozac. *Newsweek,* p. 41.

Crawford, J., Kippax, S., Onyx, J., Gault, V., & Benton, P. (1992). *Emotion and gender.* Newbury Park, CA: Sage.

Cretser, G. A., Lombardo, W. K., Lombardo, B., & Mathis, S. (1982). Reactions to men and women who cry: A study of sex differences in perceived societal attitudes versus personal attitudes. *Perceptual and Motor Skills, 55,* 479–486.

Crowther, P. (1985). Crying workshop to be offered. *The Atlantic, 5,* 42.

The crying game. (1993, October 25). *Sports Illustrated,* p. 13.

Damasio, A. R. (1994). *Descartes' error.* New York: Putnam.

Darwin, C. (1955). *Expression of the emotions in man and animals.* New York: Philosophical Library. (Original work published 1872)

Delp, M. J., & Sackeim, H. A. (1987). Effects of mood on lacrimal flow: Sex differences and symmetry. *Psychophysiology, 24,* 550–556.

Denzin, K. K. (1984). *On understanding emotion.* San Francisco: Jossey-Bass.

Diamond, J. (1993). *The third chimpanzee.* New York: HarperCollins.

Dorr, A. (1985). Contexts for experience with emotion, with special attention to television. In M. Lewis & C. Saarni (Eds.), *The socialization of emotions.* New York: Plenum Press.

Dunne, P. (1991, September 30). Men, women and tears. *Time,* p. 84.

Efran, J. S., & Spangler, T. J. (1979). Why grown-ups cry. *Motivation and Emotion, 12*(3), 63–72.

Ekman, P., Friesen, W. V., & O'Sullivan, M. (1988). Smiles when lying. *Journal of Personality and Social Psychology, 54,* 414–420.

Ellis, A., & Grieger, R. (1977). *Handbook of rational emotive therapy.* New York: Springer.

Emsley, J. (1987). Chemistry in tears. *New Scientist, 16,* 35.

Estes, J. (1994, May 30). Remembrance and restoration. *Newsweek,* p. 10.

Farrell, W. (1986). *Why men are the way they are.* New York: McGraw-Hill.

Fossey, D. (1972). Vocalizations of mountain gorillas. *Animal Behavior, 20,* 36–53.

Fox, J. L. (1985). Crying mellows some, masculinizes others. *Psychology Today, 2,* 14.

Frank, J. D. (1973). *Persuasion and healing.* Baltimore: Johns Hopkins University Press.

Freedman, J. F. (1995). *The obstacle course.* New York: Signet.

Freud, S. (1953). Interpretation of dreams. In J. Strachey (Ed. and Trans.), *The standard edition of the complete psychological works of Sigmund Freud* (Vol. 2). London: Hogarth Press. (Original work published 1900)

Freud, S. (1959). Fragment of an analysis of a case of hysteria. In *Collected papers* (Vol. 3). New York: Basic Books. (Original work published 1905)

Frey, W. H. (1985). *Crying: The mystery of tears.* Minneapolis: Winston Press.

Frey, W. H. (1992). Tears: Medical research helps explain why you cry. *Mayo Clinic Health Letter,* pp. 4–5.

Frey, W. H., Ahern, C., Gunderson, B. D., & Tuason, V. B. (1986). Biochemical behavioral and genetic aspects of psychogenic lacrimation: The unknown function of emotional tears. In F. J. Holly (Ed.), *The preocular tear film.* Lubbock, TX: Dry Eye Institute.

Frey, W. H., Hoffman-Ahern, C., Johnson, R. A., Lykken, D. T., & Tuason, V. B. (1983). Crying behavior in the human adult. *Integrative Psychiatry, 1,* 94–100.

Frijda, N. (1982). The meanings of emotional expression. In M. R. Key (Ed.), *Nonverbal communication today.* Berlin: Mouton.

Frijda, N. H. (1989). Aesthetic emotions and reality. *American Psychologist, 44,* 1546–1547.

Frye, M. (1992). Getting it right. *Signs: Journal of Women in Culture and Society, 17,* 781–793.

Fulcher, J. S. (1942). Voluntary facial expression in blind and seeing children. *Archives of Psychology, 272,* 5–49.

Gergen, K. J. (1991). *The saturated self.* New York: Basic Books.

Glantz, K., & Pearce, J. (1989). *Exiles from Eden.* New York: Norton.

Goffman, E. (1959). *The presentation of self in everyday life.* New York: Anchor.

Gold, S. R., Fultz, J., Burke, C. H., Prisco, A. G., & Willet, J. A. (1992). Vicarious emotional responses of macho college males. *Journal of Interpersonal Violence, 1*(2), 165–174.

Golub, H. L., & Corwin, M. J. (1985). A physioacoustic model of the infant cry. In B. M. Lester & C. F. Z. Boukydis (Eds.), *Infant crying: Theoretical and research perspectives.* New York: Plenum Press.

Goodenough, F. L. (1932). Expressions of emotions in a blind-deaf child. *Journal of Abnormal and Social Psychology, 27,* 328–333.

Grainger, R. D. (1991). When crying becomes a problem. *American Journal of Nursing, 4,* 15.

Green, R. L., McAllister, T. W., & Bernat, J. L. (1987). A study of crying in medically and surgically hospitalized patients. *American Journal of Psychiatry, 144*(4), 442–447.

Greenberg, L. S., & Johnson, S. M. (1988). *Emotionally focused therapy for couples.* New York: Guilford Press.

Greenberg, L. S., & Safran, J. D. (1987). *Emotion in psychotherapy.* New York: Guilford Press.

Gross, J. J., Fredrickson, B. L., & Levinson, R. W. (1994). The psychophysiology of crying. *Psychophysiology, 31,* 460–468.

Gullo, J. (1992). When grown men weep. *Premiere, 4,* 19.

Hall, H. (1987). Carry on: A cure for chronic crying. *Psychology Today, 1,* 10.

Hallock, K. (1995). Don't be afraid to cry. *American Journal of Nursing, 95,* 80.

Hands have no tears to flow, but presidents do. (1993, June 28). *Time,* p. 18.

Harkness, S., & Super, C. M. (1985). Child-environment interactions in the socialization of affect. In M. Lewis & C. Saarni (Eds.), *The socialization of emotions.* New York: Plenum Press.

Harre, R. (1986). An outline of the social constructivist viewpoint. In R. Harre (Ed.), *The social construction of emotions.* New York: Basil Blackwell.

Hastrup, J. L., Baker, J. G., Kraemer, D. L., & Bornstein, R. F. (1986). Crying and depression among older adults. *The Gerontologist, 26*(1), 91–96.

Heelas, P. (1986). Emotional talk across cultures. In R. Harre (Ed.), *The social construction of emotions.* New York: Basil Blackwell.

Heider, K. G. (1991). *Landscapes of emotion: Mapping three cultures of emotion in Indonesia.* Cambridge, England: Cambridge University Press.

Hochschild, A. P. (1983). *The managed heart: Commercialization of human feeling.* Berkeley: University of California Press.

Hoover-Dempsey, K. V., Plas, J. M., & Walston, B. S. (1986). Tears and weeping among professional women: In search of new understanding. *Psychology of Women Quarterly, 10,* 19–34.

Hunt, M. (1990). *The compassionate beast.* New York: Morrow.

Israeloff, R. (1993). Are you a crybaby? Here's why baby. *Cosmopolitan, 4,* 28.

Izard, C. E. (1991). *The psychology of emotions.* New York: Plenum Press.

James, W. (1984). The physical basis of emotion. *Psychological Review, 1,* 516–529.

Jones, S. (1992). *Crying baby, sleepless nights.* Boston: Harvard Common Press.

Karlsrud, K. (1989). The meaning of cries. *Parents, 64*(10), 224.

Katy, J. (1980). Discrepancy, arousal, and labeling: Toward a psychosocial theory of emotion. *Sociological Inquiry, 50,* 147–156.

Kemper, T. D. (1980). Sociology, physiology, and emotions. *American Journal of Sociology, 85,* 1418–1423.

King, L. A., & Emmans, R. A. (1990). Conflict over emotional expression: Psychological and physical correlates. *Journal of Personality and Social Psychology, 58*(5), 864–877.

Kirchner, J., & Goodman, E. (1993). Movies that make us sob. *Glamour, 10,* 161.

Konner, M. (1982). *The tangled wing.* New York: HarperCollins.

Kopecky, G. (1992). Have a good cry. *Redbook, 5,* 106–108.

Kottler, J. A. (1990). *Private moments, secret selves.* New York: Ballantine.

Kottler, J. A. (1991). *The compleat therapist.* San Francisco: Jossey-Bass.

Kottler, J. A. (1993). *On being a therapist* (rev. ed.). San Francisco: Jossey-Bass.

Kottler, J. A. (1994). *Beyond blame: A new way of resolving conflict in relationships.* San Francisco: Jossey-Bass.

Kupers, T. A. (1993). *Revisioning men's lives.* New York: Guilford Press.

Kutner, L. (1992, August 27). Dealing with crybabies: Children who are easily moved to tears also tend to laugh easily. *The New York Times,* p. B5.

Kutner, L. (1994, September). Cry baby. *Parents,* pp. 73–74.

Labott, S. M., Ahleman, S., Wolever, M. E., & Martin, R. B. (1990). The physiological and psychological effects of the expression and inhibition of emotion. *Behavioral Medicine, 16*(4), 182–189.

Labott, S. M., Elliot, R., & Eason, P. S. (1992). "If you love someone, you don't hurt them": A comprehensive process analysis of a weeping event in therapy. *Psychiatry, 55,* 49–62.

Labott, S. M., & Martin, R. B. (1987). The stress-moderating effects of weeping and humor. *Journal of Human Stress, 13*(4), 159–164.

Labott, S. M., & Martin, R. B. (1988). Weeping: Evidence for a cognitive theory. *Motivation and Emotion, 12*(3), 205–216.

Lacan, J. A. (1968). *Speech and language in psychoanalysis.* Baltimore: Johns Hopkins University Press.

Langlois, J. (1992, September 15). [Review of the book *Crying baby, sleepless nights: Why your baby is crying and what you can do about it*]. *Library Journal,* p. 79.

Lazarus, R. S. (1991). *Emotion and adaptation.* New York: Oxford University Press.

Lazarus, R. S., & Lazarus, B. N. (1994). *Passion and reason: Making sense of our emotion.* New York: Oxford University Press.

Lee, G. (1994). *Honor and duty.* New York: Knopf, p. 250.

Lee, K. (1994). The crying pattern of Korean infants and related factors. *Developmental Medicine and Child Neurology, 36,* 601–607.

Lendrum, S., & Syme, G. (1992). *Gift of tears: A practical approach to loss and bereavement in counselling.* London: Tavistock/Routledge.

LePage, K. E., Schafer, D. W., & Miller, A. (1992). Alternating unilateral lachrymation. *American Journal of Clinical Hypnosis, 34*(4), 255–260.

Leroy, G. (1988). Tears that speak. *Psychology Today, 8,* 2.

Lester, B. (1985). There's more to crying than meets the ear. In B. M. Lester & C. F. Z. Boukydis (Eds.), *Infant crying: Theoretical and research perspectives.* New York: Plenum Press.

Levy, R. I. (1984). Emotion, knowing, and culture. In R. A. Shweder & R. A. LeVine (Eds.), *Culture theory: Essays on mind, self, and emotion.* Cambridge, England: Cambridge University Press.

Lieberman, P. (1985). The physiology of cry and speech in relation to linguistic behavior. In B. M. Lester & C. F. Z. Boukydis (Eds.), *Infant crying: Theoretical and research perspectives.* New York: Plenum Press.

Lombardo, W. K., Cretser, G. A., Lombardo, B., & Mathis, S. L. (1983). For cryin' out loud—there is a sex difference. *Sex Roles, 9*(9), 987–995.

Lutz, C. (1985). Cultural patterns and individual differences in the child's emotional meaning system. In B. M. Lester & C. F. Z. Boukydis (Eds.), *Infant crying: Theoretical and research perspectives.* New York: Plenum Press.

MacLean, P. D. (1993). Cerebral evolution of emotion. In M. Lewis & J. M. Haviland (Eds.), *Handbook of emotions.* New York: Guilford Press.

Malatesta, C. Z., & Haviland, J. M. (1985). Signal, symbols, and socialization. In B. M. Lester & C. F. Z. Boukydis (Eds.), *Infant crying: Theoretical and research perspectives.* New York: Plenum Press.

Marlette, D. (1993). Never trust a weeping man. *Esquire, 10,* 70–71.

Marston, A., Hart, J., Hileman, C., & Faunce, W. (1984). Toward the laboratory study of sadness and crying. *The American Journal of Psychology, 97*(1), 127–131.

Martin, R. B., & Labott, S. M. (1991). Mood following emotional crying: Effects of the situation. *Journal of Research in Personality, 25,* 218–244.

Masson, J., & McCarthy, S. (1995). *When elephants weep: The emotional lives of animals.* New York: Delacorte.

Mills, C. K., & Wooster, A. D. (1987). Crying in the counselling situation. *British Journal of Guidance and Counselling, 15*(2), 125–130.

Moir, A., & Jessel, D. (1989). *Brain sex: The real difference between men and women.* London: Mandarin.

Moore, T. (1992). *Care of the soul.* New York: HarperCollins.

Moore, T. (1994). *Soulmates: Honoring the mysteries of love and relationship.* New York: HarperCollins.

Morris, D. (1977). *Manwatching: A field guide to human behavior.* New York: Abrams.

Murray, A. D. (1985). Aversiveness is in the mind of the beholder: Perception of infant crying by adults. In B. M. Lester & C. F. Z. Boukydis (Eds.), *Infant crying: Theoretical and research perspectives.* New York: Plenum Press.

Newman, J. D. (1985). The infant cry in primates: An evolutionary perspective. In B. M. Lester & C. F. Z. Boukydis (Eds.), *Infant crying: Theoretical and research perspectives.* New York: Plenum Press.

Nicholson, J. (1993). *Men and women: How different are they?* Oxford: Oxford University Press.

Odent, M. (1993). Man, the womb and the sea: The roots of the symbolism of water. *Pre- and Perinatal Psychology Journal, 7*(3), 187–193.

Okada, F. (1991). Is the tendency to weep one of the most useful indicators for depressed mood? *Journal of Clinical Psychiatry, 52*(8), 351–352.

Oswald, P. F., & Murray, T. (1985). The communicative and diagnostic significance of infant sounds. In B. M. Lester & C. F. Z. Boukydis (Eds.), *Infant crying: Theoretical and research perspectives.* New York: Plenum Press.

Pennebaker, J. W., & Roberts, T. A. (1992). Toward a his and hers theory of emotion: Gender differences in visceral perception. *Journal of Social and Clinical Psychology, 11,* 199–212.

Plas, J. M., & Hoover-Dempsey, K. V. (1988). *Working up a storm: Anger, anxiety, joy and tears on the job.* New York: Ivey Books.

Poyatos, F. (1983). *New perspectives in nonverbal communication.* Oxford: Pergamon Press.

Rice, L. N., & Greenberg, L. S. (1991). Two affective change events in client centered therapy. In J. D. Safran & L. S. Greenberg (Eds.), *Emotion, psychotherapy, and change.* New York: Guilford Press.

Roberts, M. (1987). No language but a cry. *Psychology Today, 6,* 57–58.

Rosenblatt, P. C., Walsh, R. P., & Jackson, D. A. (1976). *Grief and mourning in cross-cultural perspective.* New Haven, CT: Human Relations Area Files.

Ross, C. E., & Mirowsky, J. (1984). Men who cry. *Social Psychology Quarterly, 47*(2), 138–146.

Safran, J. D., & Greenberg, L. S. (Eds.). (1991). *Emotion, psychotherapy and change.* New York: Guilford Press.

Scheff, T. J. (1987). Two studies of emotion: Crying and anger control. *Contemporary Sociology, 16*(4), 458–460.

Scherer, K. R., Wallbott, H. G., Matsumoto, D., & Kudoh, T. (1988). Emotional experience in cultural context. In K. R. Scherer (Ed.), *Facets of emotion.* Hillsdale, NJ: Erlbaum.

Schieffelin, E. (1976). *The sorrow of the lonely and the burning of the dancers.* New York: St. Martin's Press.

Shott, S. (1979). Emotion and social life: A symbolic interactionist analysis. *American Journal of Sociology, 84,* 1317–1334.

Siegel, B. (1994). Crying in stairwells. *Journal of the American Medical Association, 272,* 659.

Signer, S. F. (1988). Pathological crying and laughter. *American Journal of Psychiatry, 145*(2), 278.

Singh, D. *A tear and a star.* Bowling Green, VA: Sawan Kirpal.

Sloboda, J. A. (1991). Music structure and emotional response: Some empirical findings. *Psychology of Music, 19*(2), 110–120.

Sturgis, A. (1995, May 20). Rarely reduced to tears. *Spectator,* pp. 18–19.

Terrace, H. (1979). *Nim: A chimpanzee who learned sign language.* New York: Washington Square Press.

Thompkins, S. S. (1962). *Affect, imagery, consciousness.* New York: Springer.

Tiwary, K. M. (1978). Tuneful weeping: A mode of communication. *Frontiers, 3*(3), 24–27.

Trilling, D. (1994, June 6). Sexual separatism. *Newsweek,* p. 12.

Udaka, F., et al. (1984). Pathologic laughing and crying treated with levodopa. *Archives of Neurology, 41*(10), 1095–1096.

Walters, K. S. (1989). The law of apparent reality and aesthetic emotions. *American Psychologist, 44,* 1545–1546.

Watzlawick, P., Beavin, J., & Jackson, D. (1967). *Pragmatics of human interaction.* New York: Norton.

Weiss, J. (1952). Crying at the happy ending. *Psychoanalytic Review, 39,* 338.

White, M., & Epston, D. (1900). *Narrative means to therapeutic ends.* New York: Norton.

Williams, D. G. (1982). Weeping by adults: Personality correlates and sex differences. *The Journal of Psychology, 110,* 217–226.

Wright, R. (1994). *The moral animal.* New York: Pantheon.

Yerkes, R. M., & Yerkes, B. N. (1929). *The great apes.* New Haven, CT: Yale University Press.

Young, J. (1982). Loneliness, depression, and cognitive therapy: Theory and application. In L. A. Peplan & D. Perlman (Eds.), *Loneliness: A sourcebook of current theory, research, and therapy.* New York: Wiley.

about the author

JEFFREY A. KOTTLER is professor of counseling and educational psychology at the University of Nevada, Las Vegas. He is the author of twenty books about therapeutic relationships and the most intimate aspects of being human.

index